FOOTSTEPS
an anthology of Walking in Wales

FOOTSTEPS

an anthology of Walking in Wales

Edited by Dewi Roberts

ISBN: 0-86381-774-2

Cover design: Sian Parri

First published in 2002 by
Gwasg Carreg Gwalch, 12 Iard yr Orsaf, Llanrwst,
Wales LL26 0EH
✆ 01492 642031   🖷 01492 641502
✆ books@carreg-gwalch.co.uk   Web site: www.carreg-gwalch.co.uk

For Arthur Smith, editor of 'Cambrensis'
who also happens to enjoy walking

Acknowledgements

Every effort has been made to contact the owners of copyright in connection with inclusions in this book, but in certain cases this has not proved possible. We apologise for this but give our assurance that any omissions will be rectified in the event of a possible reprint in the future.

The estate of William Condry and Harper Collins for an extract from 'The Natural History of Wales'.

Anthony Bailey and Jonathan Cape for an extract from 'A Walk Through Wales' (1992).

John Barnie and Gwasg Gomer for an extract from 'The Confirmation' (1992).

Seren and the individual authors for the following items; Glenda Beagan; extract from 'Seasonal Change' a story from 'The Medlar Tree' (1992): 'Tourists' and 'Rights of Way' by Ruth Bidgood; 'Walking With The Wrong Person' and 'Footprints' by John Davies': 'Nightwalk' by Christine Evans; 'Watkin Path' by Peter Finch; 'what if this road' by Sheenaugh Pugh and 'Hikers' by Catherine Fisher.

Joanna Firbank for an extract from 'A Country of Memorable Honour' by Thomas Firbank.

Article extract by Bill Bryson copyright © 2001 by Bill Bryson. Reproduced by permission of Greene and Heaton Ltd; Gwyn Morris for 'The Sacred Road' by Idris Davies.

Gillian Clarke and Carcanet for 'Waterfall'.

Constable and Robinson Ltd for excerpts from 'Journey Through Love' and 'Journey Through Britain' by John Hillaby.

Kenneth Evans and 'Country Quest' for an extract from an article; Jeremy Hooker for 'Walking the Cliff Path'.

Clyde Holmes for 'Track', 'Winter Time' and 'Guy Fawkes Night'.

Duckworth for passages from 'Late in the Day' by Carol Jones.

The Estate of Gwyn Jones for an extract from 'A Prospect of Wales' (1948).

Huw Jones for 'Journey'.

The Estate of Arthur Machen for an extract from 'Far Off Things'.

Jan Morris for a passage from 'Wales; Epic Views of a Small Country'.

Leslie Norris for 'A February Morning'.

Jim Perrin for an essay extract selected from 'A Sense of Place' edited by Roly Smith, published by Michael Joseph.

Reproduced by permission of Hodder and Stoughton Limited an extract from 'Roaming Down the Wye' by W.H. Potts.

Norman Schwenk for 'Pembrokeshire Cliff Hike': Felix de Wolf for an extract from 'A Welsh Eye' by Gwyn Thomas.

The Orion Publishing Group Ltd for 'Ninetieth Birthday' by R.S. Thomas Acknowledgement is also made to J.M. Dent as publisher.

Herbert Williams for an extract from his short story 'The Stars in Their Courses'.

Dr Raymond Garlick and Gwasg Gomer for 'Winter Walk': Gee and Son (Denbigh) for passages from 'Michael Farraday in Wales' edited by Dafydd Tomos.

William Tydeman, Alun R. Jones and the University of Wales Press for passages from 'A Pedestrian Tour of North Wales' by Joseph Hucks.

Richard George for 'Map-reading the Marches'.

Mr Sheila Williams for 'City Walk, Cardiff' by John Stuart Williams.

We also wish to thank three contributors whose items appear in print here for the first time; Dr Douglas Bassett, Siân James and Don Frampton.

It has not proved possible to contact the owners of copyright for the following titles: John Moore 'Tramping Through Wales' (Dent) and 'The Welsh Marches (Chapman and Hall); Clifford Dyment 'The Railway Game' (Dent); R.M. Lockley 'The Way to an Island' (Dent); Wilson MacArthur 'The River Conway' (Cassell); William Palmer 'More Odd Corners of North Wales' (Skeffington) and 'Wales', and 'The Flight of the Mind' edited by Nigel Nicholson and Joanne Trautman published by the Hogarth Press.

Contents

Walking with Writers

Introduction

While walking on Offa's Dyke I have encountered hikers whose facial expressions are a picture of grim-faced sufference. They come in all shapes, ages and sizes and appear, to me anyway, to be striding along this fine border footpath in order that they may tell their friends in London, Bristol or Liverpool that they have 'done' the Dyke in three or four days or whatever. Let me explain at the outset that this book is not for them.

There is a good deal in the pages that follow about the sheer pleasure of taking a walk at a time when the popularity of doing so is as strong as ever, as the avalanche of guidebooks published each year is a constant reminder. These are part of an honourable tradition, for such nineteenth century publications as *The Gossiping Guide to Wales* also achieved very high sales in their time.

It was in the late eighteenth century however, and the dawn of the Romantic period, that travellers began to arrive in Wales in significant numbers. They were drawn from what we would today term 'the chattering classes' and were largely men of leisure. It had been fashionable to tour the continent, but this proved impossible during this period due to the French wars. Wales therefore provided a convenient alternative. It was after all, and thankfully remains, a land with a different language as well as having a different history, landscape and culture. Reading their accounts today one is reminded that prior to the advent of the A470, the A55 and the A5 Wales was very much a country where the visitor might expect to encounter danger, physical discomfort, extreme weather conditions and unintelligible natives. It would be impossible to compile an anthology of this kind and to omit at least some examples of the work of this sturdy breed; Coleridge Hucks, Warner, Hazlitt et al. In each item original spellings have been retained.

Much of the material which I have gathered together is about the pleasures of walking, but the reader will also find walking in other contexts. Some of the poets included cast their nets wide in this respect. R.S. Thomas, for instance, writes of a visit to a very elderly parishioner during the period when he was the vicar of Eglwysbach, John Davies writes on taking a walk in the wrong company, Ruth Bidgood reflects on the 'naïve and scholarly wonder' of early tourists, while the nineteenth century bard Gwilym Marles, an uncle to Dylan Thomas' father, retraces the footsteps of the saints.

Passages of prose fiction will also be found here by a diverse range of writers including Charles Kingsley, Thomas Love Peacock, John Barnie, Bruce Chatwin and Herbert Williams.

In what will probably prove to be his only appearance in a Welsh anthology I am particularly glad to be able to include an item by Bill Bryson.

It will not come as a surprise to discover that I enjoy walking myself and it is this sense of enjoyment, together with the passion for literature which motivates all anthologists, which has resulted in the compilation of this book.

I end with a quotation from an item in these pages by the novelist Gwyn Thomas:

'Once you have heard the lark, known the swish of feet through hill top grass and smelt the earth made ready for the seed, you are never again going to be fully happy about the cities and towns that man carries like a crippling weight upon his back.'

Dewi Roberts
Llanrhaeadr,
Dyffryn Clwyd.

Arthur Arnold

Arnold was an inveterate long-distance walker, although biographical information about him is elusive. In his book The Way of It *he wrote of his journey across an extensive stretch of England and of 'the enjoyment of the open road'.*

In The Winding Trail *he recounts a three hundred mile hike, in the nineteen forties, though Pembrokeshire, Carmarthenshire and in to the heart of industrial Glamorganshire and Monmouthshire.*

I have selected two extracts, and in the first his veneration of Borrow is revealed.

Consulting a road map we decide to leave the highway, and take a narrow country way over elevated moorland. The gentle wind here reminds me of Borrow's picture. Can you see it?

The heath with the gentle wind passing over it, laden with scent of wild flower; Borrow, tall, young, the figure of an athlete, crowned by a head of white hair; opposite the handsome young gypsy, straight as a line, equally tall, dark flashing eye, hair like the raven's wing, and the golden light of the setting sun weaving a halo around them; and Gorgio and Romany Chal talking of the deep things of life and death. 'There's likewise a wind on the heath, brother, who would wish to die?'

There are miles of this elevated open road, rising gently to nearly 700 feet above sea level. Soon after mid-day we come to a tiny, clear, sparkling brook, and where it widens out to a miniature pond we sit down to rest and eat. Water we take from the stream. For myself, since the rough experiences of the Great War, I do not hesitate to drink from any country running water that is removed from all visible contamination, and that appears to be perfectly clean.

At the opening of the second extract Arnold is leaving the village of Magor in Gwent.

Curving is the road out of Magor, and in a matter of minutes one is in Undy; a peculiar name to a long string of uninteresting houses, mostly new.

But in half a mile they are forgotten in the joy of green and fresh open undulating farm lands. Why, even cows and sheep and horses must find life a joy here. Resting on a field gate I watch birds feeding. Starlings, blackbirds, thrushes, with the first-named easily the perkiest and most vigorous. Two things are not usual so late; larks are singing overhead, and a moment ago a blackbird alighted on the hedge nearby with a worm in his bill. He hesitated seeing me, but a sudden call from fledglings in the nest decided him, and parenthood outweighed discretion and fear.

Well done blackbird! You make is easier for me to believe that He who made you and clothed you in that silken coat of black and gave you those beautiful liquid eyes, is not deaf to the cry of His children. 'He that formed the ear, shall He not hear?'

Pleasant walking brings me though Llanvihangel and Roggiett, each with its church and small cluster of cottages, and I turn up into Severn Tunnel Junction railway station. For I have decided to ride though the Tunnel rather than take the road along the north bank of the Severn; and, also for more reasons than one, not to swim the river. Waiting for a train, the sky takes up one's interest again. It is now darker above with heavy clouds; a struggle has been going on all day, and the decision is not yet.

'A Winding Trail (1948)

Anthony Bailey

Bailey is the author of both fiction and non-fiction. In A Walk through Wales *he describes a pedestrian tour from Cardiff to Bangor.*

In the spring, the world seemed to be comprehensively thawing. It was going to be the warmest, driest summer in years. And as the glaciers dripped and the seas expanded and people in long-frozen Eastern European states felt the almost unknown thrill of fundamental political change, I felt my annual restlessness. It came with a desire to give it searoom or –more likely – landroom: it is a restlessness which can generally be appeased by a long walk. This time, I told myself, it should be a *really long walk*. I harboured deeply sequestered thoughts of a particular country that I wanted to survey and absorb something of, if only through the soles of my boots. The prickings of race memories, Celtic, British, English, Norman – though less tangible than memories of a dream – perhaps prompted me in the same direction. I took from a cupboard a tubular-framed backpack purchased at a south-east London Greenpeace jumble-sale and crammed it as concisely as I could with clothes for various altitudes and temperatures, with water flask, whisky flask, digestive biscuits, maps, compass, nylon raincoat, knife, laundry-soap powder, notebook, books for reading, language phrasebook, cheque book (no need for a passport), then made a few phone calls to friends of friends who might be helpful, patted the dog, kissed my wife, and with a cheerful 'Who knows? – I may be at least three weeks', set off. I was departing for the closest-to-hand foreign country: Wales.

A Walk through Wales (1992)

John Barnie

John Barnie wears a number of hats. He is a poet, novelist, essayist, editor of the journal 'Planet' and a blues music performer.

As he reached the top of Bryn Arw there was only the warm thin mountain air of a summer's day. The hill was like a clumsy stumbling beast, an outcrop of the Black Mountains, its upland grass bleached to straw, grey rock breaking through along the ridge. John had the sense of balancing on its shambling back. To the east the hedgerowed fields of England blazed green, fading into a distant hazy blue; to the west, ridge on ridge of the Black Mountains, rising like slow Atlantic waves, jostling in the endless thrust of the Earth, moving with the flotsam of farms and animals. Shadows of clouds grazed across them, dulling their greens, then rushed with the speed of a tide up the slope of Bryn Arw to engulf him. The hills were still and kinetic, a rolling swell on the edge of its fullness, about to crumble and break.

Once in the afternoon he disturbed a group of red grouse. Six birds had risen from the ground beneath his feet, with a snapping of wing feathers that made him cry out. His path had seemed barren, thin sunburnt grass, outcrop rock; nothing could live there. But the grouse had lain, breasts close to the ground, complete in their disguise of inanimate earth. He had triggered their panic and they scattered like shrapnel, wings beating hard, then opening out into a bow as they glided down across the slopes into bracken.

John stopped, his heart thudding. He turned and looked round the circle of the horizon. On any hill he had the sense of being a king who owned nothing: who emptied his pockets of the currency of the town. He looked down at the railway line, heading up the valley towards Hereford. A goods train steamed over it in miniature. If he were there at the line's edge he would hear the speed of its weight twanging through the track like a twisted warning, before the engine and the long line of brown rattling trucks flashed by.

Here on the height they were playthings.

from *The Confirmation* (1992)

Douglas Bassett

Dr Douglas Bassett, who now lives in retirement in Cardiff, is one of the most distinguished geologists in Wales. In 1959 he was appointed Keeper of Geology at the National Museum of Wales and eighteen years later became the Director. In this commissioned contribution he recalls his impressions of his daily walk to work from Llandaff. He walked this route daily for twenty five years, but here describes the topography as it was in the nineteen sixties.

Llandaff is a city
Cardiff is a town.
Llandaff shall stand
When Cardiff will drown.

Traditional rhyme

When I turn left at the front gate, heading eastwards and uphill towards the village, I am walking along a nearly straight line which was, in medieval times, a well-established traffic route heading for the lowest fording point of the River Taff.

As I get to the junction with Cardiff Road – the western edge of the very small borough or city of Llandaff – one of its oldest hostelries, the Malsters Arms, is on my left, the Black Lion opposite, with John Pritchard's beautiful Probate Registry next door. Pritchard, the Diocesan architect, was largely responsible for the major restoration of the Cathedral in the mid 19th century and for a number of other buildings in the village.

The non-conformist church clearly had little hope in a Cathedral village like this, but a Calvinistic Methodist Chapel still stands in the narrow terraced Chapel Street – although it is now owned by the Church in Wales.

At the southern tip of the Green, the dominant features include the massive fortified gateway of the Bishop's Castle, on the right, and the skeleton of the 13th century Bell Tower and the Preaching (or City) Cross on my left. Traditionally the cross marks the spot where Archbishop Baldwin and Giraldus Cambrensis preached the Third Crusade in 1188.

At this point the road falls away down a reasonably steep bluff, or allt, and I am given a complete view of the south prospect of the Cathedral from the two western towers to the Lady Chapel and the projecting Chapter House. The River Taff is still some distance away, but in earlier times it was much closer to the Cathedral (the 'Llan' on the River Taff) as well as being tidal up to this point. These two factors meant that the surprisingly varied stones used in the building could be brought by ship virtually to the site.

By the time I reach Western Avenue, the first of Cardiff's bypasses, I have crossed the boundary between the small and ancient ecclesiastical city and the Edwardian city of Cardiff. The two were united in 1922. As I cross the avenue the Llandaff Technical College, built on a green field site in 1953, is on one side and the studios of Television Wales and the West on the other.

At this point I enter the main section of the swathe of parkland which stretches along the river down as far as Cardiff Castle – an area of green that distinguishes the city's centre from virtually every other urban setting in Britain. First I cross Llandaff Fields, then Pontcanna Fields, and, on crossing the river by the foot-bridge at Black Weir, into the northern part of the Castle grounds or Bute Park.

This part of the walk provides a series of surprisingly long vistas, with the spire of the Cathedral to be seen between the trees behind me and the clock tower of the City Hall in front.

At this time of morning there is little traffic on Western Avenue or on Cardiff Road, which is just visible cresting the distinctive bank almost a quarter of a mile away to the right; and there is hardly anyone in the fields. The 'pastoral' nature of my surroundings is effectively highlighted in early summer when the local farmer is out training his sheepdogs in Pontcanna Fields in readiness for the regional and national trials. I leave the Castle grounds near the Welsh College of Music and Drama and step into the Civic Centre in Cathays Park. En route I cross North Road and the 'docks feeder' and the infilled course of the Glamorganshire Canal, important elements in the evolution of the city and appropriately defining the civic centre on the west. When the wind is from the east I hear the trains on the line which was originally the Taff Vale Railway. The TVR, as it became known, was responsible for the surprisingly rapid rate of Cardiff's growth.

The assemblage of striking buildings, faced with Portland Stone, arranged around a central rectangle laid out as formal gardens, has, of course, attracted widespread attention over the years, particularly in the decades prior to the Second World War. I enter between the Temple of Peace and the University of Wales Institute of Science and Technology, the origins of the former being due to the ideals of David Davies of Llandinam and the building presented by him to the Welsh people shortly before the First World War.

As I move across the top end of the avenue of elm trees-planted by Lord Bute in the late nineteenth century, the view is little different from that which the architect Dewi Prys Thomas recalled following his first visit to Cardiff in 1936, having cycled from his home in Liverpool:

'A vast urban space stretched before me towards distant domed buildings. *They were white.* Unreal to my northern eye, they shimmered in the glow of late summer – a prospect which, I felt sure, could not be bettered by the Tuileries Gardens . . . The impact of that magical first impression is indelible. It was all so much an antithesis of England's satanic mills . . . '

As I stand with the Welsh Office behind me (occupying the building erected by the Welsh Board of Health in 1938) the Welsh National War Memorial is directly ahead. The figures of a soldier, a sailor and an airman face the entrances into the sunken court within the colonnade with the fountain at the centre. The Book of Remembrance of those who fell in the Great War is on public view in the crypt of the Temple of Peace and that for the Second World War in the Main Hall of the National Museum. On my left is the 'new' building of the University College of South Wales and Monmouthshire (now University of Wales Cardiff), considered as among the church architect W.D. Caroe's best secular works. There is, naturally, no outward reflection of the complicated history of the institution nor, indeed, of any of the other buildings. But it is a pity that the College historian's comment that the College was 'built, not indeed on sand, but on a pile of debt (equal to four times the annual general income)' is not carved somewhere reasonably prominent! The building was in fact built on river gravel.

To my right is the Glamorgan County Hall, soon to become the Mid

Glamorgan County Hall, and the Registry of the University of Wales. The latter was the first building to be erected in the Park and remains the smallest. It was also the first of the five national institutions now represented in the civic centre.

By sidestepping into Museum Avenue from the central gardens – originally University Gardens and now Alexandra Gardens – and walking between the National Museum and the City Hall, I am amongst the elms that were very soon scheduled to be cut down because of the widespread disease. Myfanwy Haycock wrote her poem about these particular elms in 1938

'Nothing can be lovlier, lovlier than these.'

My daily journey of almost two miles and a quarter, ends by mounting the front steps of the Museum. This wide series of gently rising, shallow steps has had, at least since the days of the charabanc, a life of its own. In particular it acts as a very convenient venue for the arrival and departure of parties of both local people and visitors to the city with little or no connection to the Museum.

I enter the Main Hall of Yr Amgueddfa Genedlaethol around 8.00 a.m., hopefully ready for a good day's work.

Glenda Beagan

Glenda Beagan has published two accomplished short story collections, The Medlar Tree *and* Changes and Dreams *as well as a selection of poems in* Vixen.

What follows is the first half of a story entitled Seasonal Change.

The first time it was winter. February. Not cold though, really. She waited till six o'clock. Then all the people would be safe in their tall thin houses. She was afraid of her own transparency. That people could see. Light bulged from cracks in curtains, making bright oblongs on parked cars, on strips of privet. She slipped out quietly. Her mother was watching the News. In her mind's eye she saw deft fingers move over growing knitting, glasses perched low on her nose, lips softly counting.

She saw no one. It was easy. A dog barked somewhere. A cat appeared on a low wall, waiting to be fussed over, stroked, made much of. She gripped the torch in her pocket. She would not need it. An orange glow hummed over the town. As she left the flat streets and edged for the lanes, the farms, darkness did not make the sudden black shape she expected. The sky was a wedge of dark blue with still a pulse of light in it.

Her steps were quick and urgent. Strong. Telegraph poles whizzed by. Seemed to. Astonishing, this speed, this freedom. At the farm they were milking. Bold lights in the yard, the shippen doors held back, the rhythmic machines filling the night, making a focus of huddled roofs and walls. Caravans in the orchard under the great bare shape of the pear tree. Everything pared down to essentials. What did she feel? Exhilaration. Certainty.

Proper country now. A chill in the wind, a hint from the river. Her hands flex in her pockets. She brings out the torch. With deep glee she spins its light into the trees, the sycamore, its broad girth, the symmetry of its branches made spectral, gilded. She finds a child's abandon here, a kind of laughter, a bubble of it, anarchic, fierce, tinged with the joy of extremity. But she is not a child.

Over the first field. The cattle grid. She crosses it, rattling the metal bars. The track climbs steadily. Up there, high on the left, Top Farm in its fringe of poplars, its high gables peeping through twiggy swathes. Something that is neither moon nor starlight bathes the face of the house. No one lives there now, though sometimes, in daytime, it is still alive to the sound of tractors and trailers, collies yelping, boys swinging on gates. The house turns its emptiness, its serenity to the river, the whispering trees.

Over the first stile. It's muddy where she lands. Sheep move, soft grey shapes, too sleepy to bleat or warn. She has always had this ability, to move unannounced, unacknowledged among animals, as if accepted, as if part of their life, moving at a different pace, their pace, not part of the hectic life of humans. She walks with glad strides. Extravagant. The grass is longer, wetter. The sky is larger, a basin of deep sliding blue. The murmur of the river fills the air. Over the second stile. Into the lane. More mud. Stickier, then the central section, higher, firm with pebbles.

For centuries this track has led down to the ford, the only place to cross the river before the bridge was built. The first bridge. When was that? Twelfth century? She feels she is part of a pageant. An eighth century saint. A fourteenth century pilgrim. A friar, a Dominican, hooded in black. Soldiers and statesmen. Footpads. Rogues. The folk of the land. The folk blurring and blending. It's as if she hears the thumping of horses' hooves, the slow lumbering of wains, beasts driven to market. Flocks of geese. A dancing bear. Droves of children. She is glad to be saying goodbye.

There were picnics here with her own children. Years back. One more gate, a grey looming stone, the gate post, then the sloped field dips to the right, to a thicket of hazels and thorns. There, where the river makes its broad slow curve, silvery alders grow.

February Fill Dyke. That's what they say but the ground is surprisingly dry. Merely the hint of pulling earth on her shoes. There are cattle in the next field. They low softly. Her presence disturbs nothing. A waterbird, a coot, a moorhen, she can't see, moved unconcerned from the bank with only the faintest clatter. Movements, a chevron shape, on the dark water.

Everything is slowed, is stilled. Her own rage, if that's what it was, her own despair, if that's what it was, where are they now? She has walked for miles. She feels brightly alive. Tingling. Her skin is tingling. Warm with exertion while a cooling wind skims the river's smoothness. She sits on the bank, hugs her knees. Looks up at the sky's basin. Wonders why she came. Then the rain starts softly, hardly bothering to try.

The Medlar Tree (1992)

C.J. Bennett
(1800-1879)

Bennett enjoyed a varied and colourful life as an actor, and later took up photography. He also served in the navy.

There certainly is no society so interesting as that picked up by the tourist, who leaves with contempt the starched formalities of a great city behind him, and walks forth, unencumbered by care, to enjoy the society of mankind in its varied and unsophisticated nature. Every person we meet affords us information and delight; for a kindred spirit animates almost every individual whom you may chance to encounter in countries remarkable for beauties of scenery, and especially in a region like north Wales, where inns of the best kind are situated at the most convenient points, and the foot passenger is treated with as much respect as a lord in his carriage with four post horses. The landlords of inns here, think that a man may make the proper use of his legs without being a beggar; and that the costume of a pedestrian may cover the form of a gentleman. And this philanthropic conception contributes to form that happy combination, civil hosts and merry travellers.

There is not want of society, nor any difficulty in selecting that with which you are best pleased, for every evening brings in fresh comers from various quarters to the different places of rest and refreshments. The exchange of information respecting routes, the different adventures of the day, the peculiar feelings displayed in their recital, and countenances lit up with pleasure, give a degree of animation to the evening, never to be equalled in the brilliant drawing-room, the blaze of which seems to put out the eyes of reason.

The dangers incurred in traversing the dangerous road around Penmaenmawr figure in many of the tour accounts, as here:

On the following morning, we started to Aber. The coast scenery is extremely grand and passing, the promontory of Penmaen Bach, a semicircular range of mountains, stretching to the overpeering height of Penmaen Mawr, from a delightful shelter to one of the most beautiful coast retreats in North Wales.

The present road winds round the waist of Penmaenmawr, and nothing can exceed the terrors that, above and underneath it, meet the eye of the traveller. A few goats are generally seen wandering among the shingly surface; and their motions, though so light, send the loose fragments down, like the fall of a glacier. As I stood gazing on the awful depth beneath, four large pieces of rock rolled into the centre of the road, not ten yards from the place where I was standing, the smallest of which, had it touched me, would have caused instant death, or disabled me in such a manner as to have prevented my venturing upon a second tour. I turned my eyes above, and thought upon the legend of Dolbadarn; and my blood chilled to think, if, by any chance, a steed and rider should be precipitated over its brow – what a spectacle they would exhibit at its base!

A Pedestrian Tour through North Wales (1838)

Ruth Bidgood

The literary tourist Richard Warner, who is referred to in this poem, is represented in this anthology. See page 120.

Tourists

Warner, setting out eagerly from Bath
at five on a lively morning
for the inspiring rigours of Wales
with obliging C------- , equipped himself for adventure
with a rusty but respectable spencer
(good enough for North Wales, he said).
The travellers' huge pockets bulged with clothes,
maps, and little comforts; their heads were full
of Ossian, whose horrendous glooms
they were gratified to recognise
one evening on the road to Rhayader
(though Ossian had not prepared them
for the state of the road, or the shortage
of bedchambers at the 'Lion').
Romantic tourists, no doubt, perpetual
outsiders, but willing to love,
and finding much 'singular, striking
and indescribable'. They were comic
(embarrassed at being spotted
with their pedlars' pockets, by fashionable females),
but worked hard for their exaltations,
plodding twenty-five miles to Machynlleth
north over boggy mountains, or stumbling
two hours across rocks to find a guide
to Dolbadarn ruins. They were uncomplaining
on Snowdon in a thick mist (they drank milk
gratefully, but longed for brandy), and did not grumble
when, at Aberglaslyn, salmon failed to leap
(only two would even try). Who can say
that at the end of August, leaving Chepstow
for flood-tide at the ferry, they were taking
nothing real away, or that their naïve and scholarly wonder
had given nothing in return?

Rights of Way

He guardedly agrees
that the day is fine.
He wonders where I come from,
but will not ask. He thinks
I have left gates open,
and will check. Finding them shut
will not modify his mistrust.

Few make their way up here
to cross his yard between
old house and older barns; one
is too many. He feels as pain
this violation of land, his land,
by ancient custom and prescriptive right.

Diffidently, in cherishing sun,
I cross to the far gate.
Crouched by an ailing tractor,
sidelong he watches.
We are straitly buckled
into antagonistic rôles,
but I wave. Slowly
he raises a hand; turns away.

William Bingley
(1774-1823)

The Reverend Bingley developed a life-long passion for natural history. He has left two separate accounts of his journeys through the northern counties of Wales which make fascinating reading. These were published together in one volume in 1814.

A traveller on foot, if in health and spirits, has, in my opinion, many advantages over all others: of these the most essential is that complete independence of every thing but his own exertions, which will enable him, without difficulty to visit and examine various places that are altogether inaccessible to persons either in carriages or on horseback.

I was much disappointed in the walk from St Asaph to Denbigh. From remarking in the maps that it lay entirely along the vale of Clwyd, I had expected many elegant and varied prospects. The road, however, lies so low, and the vale is so wide, and so much intersected with lofty hedge-rows, that it was only in two or three places that I had any interesting prospect whatever. A woody dell, watered by the river Elwy, and ornamented with a gentleman's seat or two, pleasingly situated amongst the trees on its rising bank, afforded a picturesque scene on the right of the road, about three miles from St Asaph.

Here Bingley passes on some tips to the reader who intends to ascend Snowdon.

Welsh tourists have been much in the habit of over-rating the difficulties that are to be encountered in the journey to the summit of this mountain. To provide against these, one of them recommends a strong stick with a spike in the end as a thing absolutely necessary; another advises that the soles of the shoes be set round with large nails, and a third inveighs against attempting so arduous and so difficult an undertaking in boots. I can only say that to have nails in the shoes and to take a stick in one's hand may both be useful in their way but, if a person is in good health and spirits, he will find that he can do very well without either.

I should recommend to the traveller to allow himself sufficient time; to be upon the journey by five or six o'clock in the morning when the sun has not yet attained much power and when the air is cool and refreshing. The chief thing required is a little labour and this, by going gently along, will be rendered very easy. There is also another advantage in having plenty of time; by stopping frequently to rest himself he will be enabled to enjoy the different distance prospects as they rise above the mountains and to observe how the objects around him gradually change their appearance as he rises higher and higher. It will always be necessary to take a guide for otherwise a sudden change in the weather might render the attempt extremely perilous to a stranger. But these changes are of no consequence to the men who are in the habits of ascending the mountain very frequently, for they have marks by which they would know the path in the most cloudy weather. A sufficient supply of eatables is also absolutely necessary: the traveller will find the utility of these long before he returns.

A Tour Round North Wales (1804)

George Borrow
(1801-1881)

Wild Wales is a work which has enduring appeal. It is certainly the most popular work in the travel genre about Wales. A few years ago I pursued Borrow's route through North Wales and wrote about my experiences in The Land of Old Renown.

I have chosen two extracts from Wild Wales. *The first of these reflects the rigidity of the Methodist outlook in the nineteenth century.*

'Is that gentlewoman your wife?'
   'She is no gentlewoman, sir, but she is my wife.'
   'Of what religion are you?'
   'We are Calvinistic-Methodists, sir.'
   'Have you been to chapel?'
   'We are just returned, sir.'
Here the woman said something to her husband, which I did not hear, but the purport of which I guessed from the following question which he immediately put.
   'Have you been to chapel, sir?'
   'I do not go to chapel; I belong to the Church.'
   'Have you been to church, sir?'
   'I have not – I said my prayers at home, and then walked out.'
   'It is not right to walk out on the Sabbath day, except to go to church or chapel.'
   'Who told you so?'
   'The law of God, which says you shall keep holy the Sabbath day.'
   'I am not keeping it unholy.'
   'You are walking about, and in Wales when we see a person walking idly about, on the Sabbath day, we are in the habit of saying "Sabbath breaker, where are you going?"'
   'The Son of Man walked through the fields on the Sabbath day, why should I not walk along the roads?'
   'He who called Himself the Son of Man was God, and could do what He pleased, but you are not God.'

'But He came in the shape of a man to set an example. Had there been anything wrong in walking about on the Sabbath day, He would not have done it.'

Here the wife exclaimed, 'How wordly-wise these English are!'

'You do not like the English,' said I.

'We do not dislike them,' said the woman; 'at the present they do us no harm, whatever they did of old.'

'But you still consider them,' said I, 'the seed of Y Sarfes cadwynog, the coiling serpent.'

'I should be loth to call any people the seed of the serpent,' said the woman.

'But one of your great bards did,' said I.

'He must have belonged to the Church, and not to the chapel then,' said the woman. 'No person who went to chapel would have used such bad words.'

In the second extract Borrow ascends Snowdon with Henrietta, his step-daughter.

. . . having engaged a young lad to serve as guide, I set out with Henrietta to ascend the hill, my wife remaining behind, not deeming herself sufficiently strong to encounter the fatigue of the expedition.

Pointing with my finger to the head of Snowdon towering a long way from us in the direction of the east, I said to Henrietta: 'Dacw Eryri, yonder is Snowdon. Let us try to get to the top. The Welsh have a proverb: "It is easy to say yonder is Snowdon; but not so easy to ascend it." Therefore I would advise you to brace up your nerves and sinews for the attempt.'

We then commenced the ascent, arm in arm, followed by the lad, I singing at the stretch of my voice a celebrated Welsh stanza, in which the proverb about Snowdon is given, embellished with a fine moral, and which may thus be rendered:

'Easy to say, "Behold Eryri",'
But difficult to reach its head;
Easy for him whose hopes are cheery
To bid the wretch be comforted.'

We were far from being the only visitors to the hill this day; groups of people, or single individuals, might be seen going up or descending the path as far as the eye could reach. The path was remarkably good, and for some way the ascent was anything but steep. On our left was the vale of Llanberis, and on our other side a broad hollow, or valley of Snowdon, beyond which were two huge hills forming part of the body of the grand mountain, the lowermost of which our guide told me was called Moel Elia, and the uppermost Moel y Cynghorion. On we went until we had passed both these hills, and come to the neighbourhood of a great wall of rocks constituting the upper region of Snowdon, and where the real difficulty of the ascent commences. Feeling now rather out of breath we sat down on a little knoll with our faces to the south, having a small lake near us, on our left hand, which lay dark and deep, just under the great wall.

Here we sat for some time resting and surveying the scene which presented itself to us, the principal object of which was the north-eastern side of the mighty Moel y Cynghorion, across the wide hollow or valley, which it overhangs in the shape of a sheer precipice some five hundred feet in depth. Struck by the name of Moel y Cynghorion, which in English signifies the hill of the counsellors, I inquired of our guide why the hill was so called, but as he could afford me no information on the point I presumed that it was either called the hill of the counsellors from the Druids having held high consultation on its top, in time of old, or from the unfortunate Llywelyn having consulted there with his chieftains, whilst his army lay encamped in the vale below.

Getting up we set about surmounting what remained of the ascent. The path was now winding and much more steep than it had hitherto been. I was at one time apprehensive that my gentle companion would be obliged to give over the attempt; the gallant girl, however, persevered, and in little more than twenty minutes from the time when we arose from our resting-place under the crags, we stood, safe and sound, though panting, upon the very top of Snowdon, the far-famed Wyddfa.

'Here,' said I to Henrietta, 'you are on the top crag of Snowdon, which the Welsh consider, and perhaps with justice, to be the most remarkable crag in the world; which is mentioned in many of their old wild romantic tales, and some of the noblest of their poems, amongst others in the "Day of Judgement", by the illustrious Goronwy Owen, where it is brought forward in the following manner:

Ail i'r ar ael Eryri
Cyfartal hoewal a hi.

'The brow of Snowdon shall be levelled with the ground, and the eddying waters shall murmur round it.'

Wild Wales (1862)

Bill Bryson

Years ago, not long after I first arrived in Britain, I remember wandering into a bookshop and being startled to find a section devoted to walking guides. Where I came from we didn't walk much, but at least we could do it without instructions. Only gradually did I come to realise that in Britain there are two types of walking – the everyday sort with which I was familiar and a more earnest type involving sturdy boots, maps, rucksacks and, yes, walking guides.

Soon afterwards, I had my first encounter with members of this latter group. Early on a cold, wet Sunday morning, just outside Hay-on-Wye, I passed dozens of people kitting up to take to the hills. Across the way dozens more could be seen vanishing into the mists clinging to a sheer eminence called Hay Bluff. Never having seen anything like this before – people venturing out in dire weather to clamber up steep hills in the belief that there could be some pleasure in it – I watched for some minutes, and concluded that they were suffering a sort of derangement.

I was right, of course. Walkers are deranged. But with the passage of time I also learned that it was a derangement worth having. Rambling is wonderful. It's invigorating, it's absurdly healthy, it costs next to nothing and there is no better way to see and luxuriate in the subtle and infinite beauty of nature.

So when I was asked if I would care to unfurl my lower limbs and see if they still possessed life enough to convey me through one of the most beguiling corners of Britain, I was all ears. When I further learned that my route was to be the ancient linear wonder that is Offa's Dyke – the very path on which I saw those people at Hay Bluff years before – I agreed with alacrity. Not until a moment later was I struck by the thought that these were the very hills that had for centuries thwarted Romans and Anglo-Saxons alike, and allowed the Welsh to maintain their separate identity.

'It's not too hard, is it?' I asked.

'Oh, no,' said Roger Thomas, the amiable and persuasive editor of *A View of Wales*, before adding with a breezy and enigmatic air: 'Well, not for someone of your experience anyway.'

Thus it was that I was to be found, one unseasonably warm spring afternoon, puffing my way up a steep hill out of Chepstow, and giving thanks that I had not committed to doing the whole path at once. From end to end Offa's Dyke Path runs 177 miles, from the Severn Estuary at Chepstow to the Irish Sea at Prestatyn, roughly – sometimes literally – following the border between England and Wales. My assignment was to walk the first 80 miles to Knighton. The southern section is relatively easy compared with the wilder northern stretches – though 'relatively' is a crucial word here for there are some steep climbs and long hauls between villages.

For all its venerable grandeur, surprisingly little is known about the origin or purpose of Offa's Dyke. Traditionally, it is ascribed to King Offa of Mercia, who in the late 8th century decreed that an earthen barrier be built along the border between Wales and his own realm next door. Because of its erratic nature – rising along some stretches to commanding heights of 20 ft or more, but elsewhere standing as little more than a low hedgebank, and in yet others disappearing altogether – historians cannot agree on whether it served as a defensive barrier or merely boundary marker. In the 1960s, some enterprising souls decided to make it into a long-distance footpath. Llwybr Clawdd Offa, as it is known in Welsh, opened officially in July 1971.

It may not be the longest or best-known footpath in the UK, but surely none can offer more varied or reliably comely scenery. An hour or so after setting off from Chepstow I entered a deep and arrestingly beautiful wood on the edge of limestone cliffs, with frequent views of the River Wye, sparkling and languid, some 200 ft below. Here I caught my first glimpse of the dyke, a wandering hummock of earth three or four feet high, not terribly imposing just here but clearly ancient. Finally, at a lookout spot called Shorn Cliff rock, I got the supreme payoff: a distant prospect of the ruins of Tintern Abbey basking in the mellow light of late afternoon.

As I stood there, a fellow walker came along. We stood in

silence for a few moments savouring the outlook.

'Do you walk this path much?' I asked after a minute.

'Not much. I've come down from Hereford for a few days.'

'I just wondered if it was always this quiet. I haven't seen anybody in two hours.'

He smiled. 'I haven't seen anybody since breakfast.'

We considered this for some moments. 'Nice, isn't it?' I said.

'Mmmmm,' he agreed.

Thirty minutes later, courtesy of a side path through the woods to Tintern, I was checking into the welcoming confines of the Parva Farmhouse Hotel. A stroll through the village to view the abbey, a pint in an old stone pub, and a hearty dinner at the Parva completed a more or less perfect introduction to the path.

Three things, if you ask me, make a perfect walk: good weather, good scenery and good company.

A View of Wales (2001)

Idris Caffrey

Pacing Backward

First, a winding lane
wedged hard into winter

Then tall hedgrows
heavy with rose hips;
blood red
against the snow

Next, fresh footprints
alone, but sure
which I follow
blindly
over the stile,
across the sweep of fields.

Lastly, I turn,
back from an unknown end –
to the safety
of a beginning.

Bruce Chatwin

Chatwin was one of the outstanding English writers of the nineteen eighties and all his works were meticulously researched. When he was writing On the Black Hill, *for example, he lived in the Welsh border country near Hay for about a year.*

The twins loved to go on walks with their grandfather, and had two particular favourites – a 'Welsh walk' up the mountain, and an 'English walk' to Lurkenhope Park.

The 'Welsh walk' was only practical in fine weather. Often, they would set out in sunshine, only to come home soaked to the skin. And equally often, when walking down to Lurkenhope, they would look back at the veil of grey rain to the west while, overhead, the clouds broke into blue and butterflies fluttered over the sunlit cow-parsley.

On the Black Hill (1982)

Gillian Clarke

Gillian Clarke, who lives on a smallholding in West Wales, is one of the finest Welsh poets writing in English.

Waterfall

We parked the car in a dusty village
That sat sideways on a hill over the coal.
We heard a rag and bone man
And a curlew. The sun for the first time
Put a warm hand across our shoulders
And touched our winter faces.

We saw summer, one lapwing to go.
Her mate was in the sky already,
Turning over, black, white-bellied,
While she, looking browner near the ground,
Tidied the winter from her crisp field.

We climbed the mountain, crossed the round
Of it, following the marshland down to the gorge.
The water was gathering minutely everywhere
Knowing its place and its time were coming.
The fall like a silk fringe distantly whispered.

Down over the boulders in the death bed
Of an old river, through thin birches and oaks,
Going where the water went, into the multitude
Of the shouting streams, no longer speaking
To each other, silenced by what the water said.

Closer to crisis the air put cold silk
Against our faces and the cliffs streamed
With sun water, caging on every gilded
Ledge small things that flew by mistake
Into the dark spaces behind the rainbows.

The path led me under the fall to feel
The arc of the river and the mountain's exact
Weight; the roar of rain and lapwings
Leaving; water-beat, heart-fall in accord,
Curlew-call, child-cry on the drum's skin
Distinguished from the inmost thoughts of rivers.

We cage our response in the roar, defer
Decision while water falls. It gathers its life
On our behalf, leaps for us, its chords
Of change that curve across the cliffs
Are only, after all, an altering of level
To where it belongs, though the falling appals.

C.F. Cliffe

It seems a work of supererogation (exceeding what is required) to
offer a word of advice to the vigorous and numerous class of
explorers who annually take to the road with knapsack or fishing-
basket on back, and staff in hand; yet we have known and heard of
so many cases in which a Welsh tour has been entered upon either

in an absurd costume, or without due provision for the proper protection of the outer man against wet weather or rough roads, that a few words of advice from an old campaigner may not be thrown away. Pedestrians ought to penetrate the wilds and nooks of the country, and be prepared to face soaking days. A really good pair of shoes is the best desideratum. Let the soles be thick and broad through-out, with copper sprigs, and double upper-leathers, of first-rate pliable materials. Most fishermen don't mind their feet wet; but we recommend them to have moderately-high ankle-boots on the above construction, to button easily, not lace. Pedestrians will find these boots not despisable. Such shoes or fishing-boots as we indicate cannot be got cheap, and they should be seasoned a little beforehand. It is hardly necessary to tell those who walk, to economise the weight they have to carry as much as possible: narrow blue-striped shirts are the most useful; and by all means wear the universal light 'Jim Crow' hat. Do not commence a tour, as many do, in old fragile clothes. A shooting jacket is best, especially on account of its pockets. If you can carry out a plan of sending a carpet-bag a-head to certain points, you will reap comfort therefrom; and will be able to manage with a very light load of personal luggage. The majority, however, make up their minds to carry a regular knapsack. A strong, useful umbrella, capable of being converted into a walking stick, will be found anything but despisable by pedestrians, for the light repellent mackintosh, if worn for any length of time, exhausts, and you may be obliged to walk through heavy rain for many hours. We altogether denounce the use of Regent Street boots and thin shoes in this rough country; the first wet day, or the first bit of turbary (peatbog), will make decided converts to this opinion.

The readiest restorative for bruised feet is hot water, with salt in it; and tallow has been found a valuable healer by many foot-sore pedestrians.

Modern remedies may come in impressive packaging but, for the walker, the problem of sore feet is a perpetual one.

The Cambrian Tourist (1814)

Samuel Taylor Coleridge
(1771-1834)

As a young man Coleridge accompanied his undergraduate friend Joseph Hucks on an extensive walking tour of north Wales. Here he describes the loss of his faithful walking stick at Abergele and what followed.
See also Joseph Hucks. (Page 74)

. . . Just before I quitted Cambridge I met a countryman with a strange walking stick, five feet in length. I eagerly bought it and a most faithful servant it has proved to be. My sudden affection for it has mellowed into settled friendship. On the morning of our leaving Abergele just before our final departure I looked for the stick in the place where I had left it overnight. It was gone! I alarmed the house. No one knew anything of it. In the flurry of anxiety I sent for the crier of the town and gave him the following to cry about the town and on the beach, which he did with a gravity for which I am indebted to his stupidity.

'Missing from the *Bee Inn*, Abergele, a curious walking stick. On one side it displays the head of an eagle . . . On the other side is the portrait of the owner in wood work . . . If any gentleman or lady has fallen in love with the above described stick and secretly carried it off, he or she is hearby earnestly admonished to conquer a passion, the contiuance of which must prove fatal to his or her honesty; and if the said stick has slipped into such gentlemans or ladies hands through inadvertence, he, or she, is required to rectify the mistake with all convenient speed. God save the King.'

Abergele is a fashionable Welsh watering place and so singular a proclamation excited no small crowd on the beach, among the rest a lame old gentleman in whose hands I espied my stick. The old gent, who lodged at our inn, felt great confusion, and walked homeward, the solemn crier before him, and a various cavalcade behind . . . He made his lameness an apology for borrowing my stick . . . Thus it ended . . . '

A Pedestrian Tour of North Wales (1795)
edited by William Tydeman and Alun Jones

William Condry
(1918-1998)

William Condry spent much of his life in mid Wales and for many years contributed the 'Country Diary' column to The Guardian. *He wrote many books on natural history and rural life, among them the excellent 'The Natural History of Wales'.*

I had come up through the mist by way of Cwm Idwal, following a track grievously worn by years of trampling. A line of girls, despite their orange waterproofs, were only dim shapes before me along the nature trail round the lake. They were, I suppose, a school party out to study the lake vegetation (the water lobelia *(Lobelia dortmanna)* still hung a few last violet flowers above the surface). Perhaps too they intended to look for geological features and were hoping that the fog would lift to let them see how beautifully the rocks are downfolded in the cliffs of this cwm.

It was then that it began to rain heavily and if I'd been alone I daresay I would have turned back, discouraged by the water seeping coldly down my neck. But if these girls could press on through the murk in such earnest pursuit of knowledge what excuse had I for giving up? And as we went on, a quite marvellous thing happened. Out of the fog and the rain from somewhere up near the crags of the Devil's Kitchen, which the Welsh call Twll Du *(black chasm)*, there swept a flock of large black birds all calling with excitement – a rather dreamlike experience for me because in my many visits to Cwm Idwal I had never seen more than two or three choughs there before. And now here were thirty of them settling on rocks on both sides of the trail or walking tamely about the sheep-nibbled sward.

Sadly I observed that the crocodile of girls had not paused at all, not one pair of eyes had turned to look at the birds, no ears had heeded the cheering calls. For these children, as also for their teacher, these lovely, noisy crows of the mountains with their sensitive, ant-seeking, bright-red bills and their equally striking red legs, just did not exist. But this lapse we must forgive because Cwm Idwal is classic ground for lack of observation. Here in his time came Charles Darwin and totally missed what is so obvious to any schoolchild today (once it is pointed out) – that this cwm is one huge piece of evidence, in the shape of moraines, scratched stones, perched boulders, screes and cirques, that a vast weight and depth of ice and frozen rocks once forced a way through here and down to Ogwen and beyond.

From the lake I turned up the slithering, crumbling track that goes for the Devil's Kitchen, a track that bore me laboriously upwards through a wilderness of mist and block scree until quite abruptly the cliffs were right overhead. I looked up and up the vertical grey walls and saw how, as nearly always, the plants grew thickest round the lower skirts – luxurious waving sheets of lady's mantle *(Alchemilla vulgaris)*, roseroot *(Sedum rosea)*, northern bedstraw *(Galium boreale)* and others that are faithful to ledges where perennial water comes oozing from deep in the rock, collecting nutritious minerals on its way. Up higher the cliffs looked harder, showing no spring lines, and plant life was very much sparser. Yet even up there a scatter of rowan trees *(Sorbus aucuparia)* (planted in the droppings of ring ouzels?) had managed to anchor themselves.

For twenty minutes the rain had eased but now it became torrential and I crouched from it under an overhang. A group of heavily rucksacked hill walkers clattered past down the scree hurrying to get out of the weather. One of them shouted to me that conditions on top were 'just terrible'. Then their figures faded into the mist below and I was alone with the lichened rocks, the dripping mosses and the rain. It was rather special rain this, being the first I had seen for many weeks, the lowlands having had a long spell of drought. But when I got home that night I found the world down there just as parched and dusty as ever. So perhaps it was worth all the water down my neck to be reminded how unique is the mountain weather and why it is that the mountain plants keep so happy, green and flowering in a summer when the rest of the world is in agony from sunburn and thirst.

The Natural History of Wales (1992)

Charles Darwin
(1809-1882)

As a young man Darwin made a geological tour of North Wales and this was to have a considerable influence on his subsequent thinking.

At Capel Curig I left Sedgwick and went in a straight line by compass and map across the mountains to Barmouth, never following any track unless it coincided with my course. I thus came on some strange wild places and enjoyed much this manner of travelling. I visited Barmouth to see some Cambridge friends who were reading there, and thence returned to Shrewsbury and to Maer for shooting; for at that time I should have thought myself mad to give up the first days of partridge-shooting for geology or any other science.

Autobiography

Idris Davies
(1905-1953)

This major Anglo-Welsh poet was born into a mining family and was employed on the coal face at the age of fourteen. In 1926 he began his training as a teacher and taught at a number of schools.

His is very much the voice of a radical and the work by which he is best remembered was directly inspired by the decline of the economy in the Valleys which led to so much social deprivation.

The Sacred Road

They walked this road in seasons past
When all the skies were overcast,
They breathed defiance as they went
Along these troubled hills of Gwent.

They talked of justice as they strode
Along this crooked mountain road,
And dared the little lords of Hell
So that the future should be well.

Because they did not count the cost
But battled on when all seemed lost,
This empty ragged road shall be
Always a sacred road to me.

John Davies

John Davies' poetic voice is very much his own and he has drawn his material from both Welsh and American sources. He lives at Prestatyn and spends much of his time carving birds from wood.

Walking with the Wrong Person

Greenscapes terminally beautiful wince
welcome. They know him. They've known him since
he started talking. Wind fiddled
with metal sheds back there, sheep stirred
slate xylophones. Both half-heard.
Irritated, a hiccuping grouse slid
off. I can't. What it is, he has become
his missing Walkman. There's space to fill –
so air swells as the packed coast spills
through him its chatter, even wind struck dumb
at the shaft where questions took their toll.
'What did you expect, a ladder?
Some trainee rockman with his dad?'
I knew what could have filled that hole.

A boulder waited like an owl upstairs
over Llyn Geirionydd. One swoop, that's all.
Or the muscular, brown-armed waterfall
could have bent and . . . Hell, nature doesn't care.
He won't switch off and it's miles from here,
miles, the burial mound at Tomen-y-Mur.

The next poem is about a walk near Betws-y-coed and what John Davies describes as 'the enviable confidence of a previous generation'. Rhiwddolion is a ghost village of ruined cottages.

Footprints

O.S. maps are fine except in forestry
where paths breed then forget,
having trees to get to, trees to see.

Each seemed the least travelled by.
They made no difference till one
gave me a shot of field and sky.

Rhiwddolion was not lost, Sprawled
houses measured the distance
between forestry and stone walls

where doorways wide enough to say
'They've gone' had ferns on mantelpieces,
draped boughs of another washday,

flicker on burned-out hearths.
Slate slabs crossed a field
like giant footprints: the one path

still went to chapel, straight.
By the time I left, there was just
that well-heeled shine of slate.

Conifers loomed. Keeping confidence
intact through shadowy twists
and times takes a lot of ignorance.

W. Watkin Davies

Even the Welsh farmer is marvellously indulgent to trespassers. Of course, he will not tolerate injury to his crops of wheat, barley, or oats, nor is he pleased to behold people wading knee-deep through his hay, or leaving gates open for animals to stray out of their proper enclosures; but when none of those evil things are being done, you may clamber over stiles, follow any paths, or even walk across fields, without let or hindrance. Such hospitable behaviour is necessarily based upon confidence in the considerate demeanour of the trespasser; and I have been told more than once of late by farmers, that the tourist of to-day is not so considerate as him of former days; he is less careful to shut gates, he pulls down loose stones from the mountain walls, he tramples down infant crops, and perpetrates other enormities of that kind. Should such carelessness become the characteristic of tourists, the inevitable will follow: farmers will erect their warning signs, and permission will no longer be given to walk, save where the law allows. I trust that the comparatively small number of delinquents will take warning in time; for if they disregard it, not they alone will have to pay the penalty, but all the hosts of well-behaved persons who derive such supreme pleasure from freely rambling over the farms of Wales.

A Wayfarer in Wales (1930)

Thomas De Quincey
(1785-1859)

De Quincey's Confessions of an English Opium Eater *is largely autobiographical. In it he recalls his flight from Manchester Grammar School at the age of sixteen. Subsequently he wandered through parts of North Wales enjoying a new found sense of freedom.*

. . . it has often struck me that a world-wearied man, who sought for the peace of monasteries separated from their gloomy captivity – peace and silence such as theirs combined with the large liberty of nature – could not do better than revolve amongst these modest inns in the five northern Welsh counties of Denbigh, Montgomery, Carnarvon, Merioneth and Cardigan. Sleeping, for instance, and breakfasting at Carnarvon; then, by an easy nine-mile walk, going forwards to dinner at Bangor, thence to Aber – nine miles; or to Llanberis; and so on for ever, accomplishing seventy to ninety or one hundred miles in a week. This, upon actual experiment, and for week after week, I found the most delightful of lives. Here was the eternal motion of winds and rivers, or of the Wandering Jew liberated from the persecution which compelled him to move, and turned his breezy freedom into a killing captivity. Happier life I cannot imagine than this vagrancy, if the weather were but tolerable, through endless successions of changing beauty, and towards evening a courteous welcome in a pretty rustic home – that having all the luxuries of a fine hotel (in particular some luxuries * that are almost sacred to Alpine regions), was at the same time liberated from the inevitable accompaniments of such hotels in great cities or at great travelling stations – viz, the tumult and uproar. Life on this model was but too delightful; and to myself especially, that am never thoroughly in health unless when having pedestrian exercise to the extent of fifteen miles at the most, and eight to ten miles at the least. Living thus, a man earned his daily enjoyment. But what did it cost? About half a guinea a day: whilst my boyish allowance was not a third of this. The flagrant health, health boiling over in fiery rapture, which ran along, side by side, with exercise on this scale, whilst all the while from morning to night I was inhaling mountain air, soon passed into a hateful scourge. Perquisites to servants and a bed would have absorbed the whole of my weekly guinea. My policy therefore was, if the autumnal air was warm enough, to save this expense of a bed and the chambermaid by sleeping amongst ferns or furze upon a hillside; and perhaps with a cloak of sufficient *weight* as well as compass, or an Arab's burnoose, this would have been no great hardship. But then in the daytime what an oppressive burden to carry! So perhaps it was as well that I had no cloak at all. I did, however, for some weeks try the plan of carrying a canvas tent manufactured by myself, and not larger than an ordinary umbrella: but to pitch this securely I found difficult; and on windy nights it became a troublesome companion. As winter drew near, this bivouacking system became too dangerous to attempt. Still one may bivouack decently, barring rain and wind, up to the end of October. And I counted, on the whole, that in a fortnight I spent nine nights abroad. There are, as perhaps the reader knows by experience, no jaguars in Wales – nor pumas – nor anacondas – nor (generally speaking) any Thugs. What I feared most, but perhaps only through ignorance of zoology, was, lest, whilst my sleeping face was upturned to the stars, some one of the many little Brahminical-looking cows on the Cambrian hills, one or other, might poach her foot into the centre of my face.

Confessions of an English Opium-Eater (1821)

John Dyer
(1700-1758)

John Dyer lived at Aberglasney, close to the Carmarthenshire village of Llangathen in the Towy Valley. The house and grounds of this fine house have been restored within the last few years. Grongar Hill lies some three miles to the west of Llandeilo.

Dyer's poem is widely regarded as one of the finest topographical poems written about Wales.

Up Grongar Hill I labour now,
And catch at last his Bushy Brow.
Oh! how fresh, how pure the Air!
Let me breathe a little here.
Where am I, Nature? I descry
Thy Magazine before me lie!
Temples! – and Towns! – and Tow'rs! – and Woods!
And Hills! – and Vales! – and Fields! – and Floods!
Crowding before me edg'd around
With naked Wilds, and barren Ground.
See below the pleasant Dome,
The Poet's Pride, the Poet's Home,
Which the Sun-Beams shine upon,
To the Even, from the Dawn.
See her Woods where *Eccho* talks,
Her Gardens trim, her Terras Walks,
Her Wildernesses, fragrant Brakes,
Her gloomy Bowers, and shining Lakes.
Keep, ye Gods, this humble seat
For ever pleasant, private, neat.
See yonder Hill, uprising steep,
Above the River slow and deep:
It looks from hence a Pyramid,
Beneath a verdant Forest hid;
On whose high Top there rises great,
The mighty Remnant of a Seat,
An old green Tow'r, whose batter'd Brow
Frowns upon the Vale below.
    Look upon that flow'ry Plain,
How the Sheep surround their Swain.

How they crowd to hear his Strain!
All careless, with his Legs across,
Leaning on a Bank of Moss,
He spends his empty Hours at play,
Which fly as light as Down away.
    And there behold a bloomy Mead,
A Silver Stream, a Willow Shade,
Beneath the Shade a *Fisher* stand,
Who, with the Angle in his Hand,
Swings the nibling Fry to Land.
    In Blushes the descending Sun
Kisses the Streams, while slow they run;
And yonder Hill remoter grows,
Or dusky Clouds do interpose.
The Fields are left, the lab'ring Hind
His weary Oxen does unbind;
And vocal Mountains, as they low,
Re-eccho to the Vales below.
The jocund Shepherds piping come,
And drive the Herd before 'em home;
And now begin to light their Fires,
Which send up Smoke in curling Spires!
While, with light Hearts, All homeward tend
To *Aberglasney* I descend.
But, Oh! how bless'd wou'd be the Day,
Did I with *Clio* pace my way,
And not alone, and solitary stray.

from *Grongar Hill (1726)*

Clifford Dyment
(1914-1970)

Dyment is primarily remembered as a poet. In 1962 he published his autobiography The Railway Game *in which he recalled his early childhood in Caerleon.*

My mother's father was a great walker and a great man for the countryside; my father was neither. Nevertheless, he set out after them; he'd decided to be with my mother that day and be with her he would. He followed the elderly man and the young woman with unfaltering tenacity, tracing their route by inquiries at cottages and public houses and by noting places where my grandfather had plucked wild herbs and flowers. In the late evening my mother and grandfather arrived home; there, hours afterwards, my father caught them up; he had taken exactly the same walk as they had, but had taken it many miles in their rear.

The Railway Game (1962)

Christine Evans

Christine Evans lives in a cottage near Aberdaron and spends much of the summer each year on Ynys Enlli (Bardsey).

Night Walkers

The sea is
a great ear turned to listen.

Soft paws of cloud
knead the moon
the night sky purrs
and presses closer.

We tread soft as mist
so small the dark could breathe us in
our thoughts bleached paler
than dandelion seeds

so when the world stirs
and shifts its weight
we see the ocean flash with fire
twice cooled to silver

but not one of the three of us
points or cries out.

John Evans
(1768-1812)

The day was drawing fast to a close when several roads appeared before us; we were at a loss which to take, and not being sufficiently acquainted with the country to travel after dark without being well instructed, I accosted a little meanly dressed man who happened just at the time to be passing, in order to ascertain the way to Caerwent; he stopped when I put the question to him, and after a pause, inquired, whence we came; I said from Chepstow; 'Oh! then,' replied he, assuming a degree of consequence, 'gentlemen, you are leaving Caerwent, for the place you come from is all that remains of it,' and without further ceremony made off, leaving us not a jot wiser than we were before; although not much pleased with the joke, we could not refrain from laughing most heartily at the important air of this South Walian antiquary, who, no doubt, imagined he had on this occasion displayed great wit, as well as judgement. A gentleman riding by shortly afterwards, very politely inquired if we wished to be directed in our road; upon our answering in the affirmative, he obligingly gave us full information, and by eight o'clock we were tracing the tesselated pavement in Caerwent: but little is now to be seen: a few of the small square stones are all that remain of this once elegant specimen of Roman ingenuity.

When first discovered, in the year 1777, it was inclosed with a wall by the proprietor of the land; but from neglect, and the depredations committed by visitors, it has been reduced to the state in which we found it, overgrown with grass and weeds! Some of the white pebbles we brought away with us, which, had the pavement been entire, or any connected part been in preservation, we should have deemed almost sacrilege to have moved. Retiring from hence, not a little disappointed, we hastened to our nightly abode.

In this, our first day's walk, you will perceive that we completed twenty-one miles, which, do us the credit to acknowledge, was not amiss for such young foot travellers. I will, however, own to you that I felt rather fatigued, and was pleased at reaching the place of entertainment, although the external appearance of the house did not give us very sanguine hopes of meeting with good cheer; nor indeed were we mistaken, for on the first survey on entering, we found but little comfort was to be had within; however, we must do our landlady the justice to say, that she really endeavoured to make things agreeable. Indeed, we should not have quitted Caerwent altogether dissatisfied, had the *fleas* been a little more merciful: neither my friend nor myself slept during the night, for the movement of that merry race completely dispelled the soporific effect which a lengthened journey had created.

Three Days Excursion from Bristol to Llandogo (1815)

. . . our guide prognosticated an approaching storm: we halted, and deliberated what was best to be done: but being rather more than half way towards Bedd Kelert, deliberation only served to remind us of our unpleasant situation. To retread our steps would have been attended with equal inconvenience as proceeding. The country afforded no shelter; no vestige of a hut; nor was it to be expected in a country devoid of vegetation. The darkness momentarily increased, the misty clouds left their towering heights, and gaining strength by approximating towards the heavier ones beneath, soon became formidable from coalition. The winds became clamorous from the West and North; and, meeting with currents from the mountain vistas, soon blew a hurricane. All foreboded a dismal issue. The guide forgot his usual gaiety and loquacity, and, began to shake, and mutter a few inarticulate sounds. Despairing of making our escape, we relaxed in our exertions, and became less quick and firm in our steps: the very beasts shook their heads and snorted, as though sensible of the perilous situation.

A general torpor at length seized the whole party; and visibly panic-struck we patiently waited the assailing elements; like mariners, who after every effort to save the vessel proves abortive, give up their toil in despair, and patiently look for the coming destruction.

A general gloom, like that of a total eclipse, pervaded the whole atmosphere: the diversified mountain scenery we had before admired, had entirely vanished. Heaven and earth seemed blended together: the crumbling strata and shivering rock beneath our feet, afforded us the only vestiges of the latter; while in the former cloud dashed against cloud in angry conflict. To this war of elements, succeeded the fiercest torrents of rain that the imagination can conceive: to say it *poured*, would be to trifle with language: no words are adequate to a description of the storm. To those who have seen a water-spout at sea, the conception may be easy; but to those who have not, we can only say, that we appeared in the situation of persons placed under one of those mountain cataracts before described, with its waters rushing down upon our heads. To those who never have visited alpine countries, no adequate description can be given; and to those who are familiar with them, this colouring will appear extremely faint.

Impelled by imperious necessity to adopt every method for self-preservation, after being frequently beaten down, we had recourse to crossing arms and joining shoulders; closing like wrestlers for support.

Letters written during a
Tour through North Wales in 1798 (1804)

Kenneth Evans

September sun-light filtered through the dense mass of oaks, beeches, birch and fir, interspersed with holly, hazel and ash, throwing spears of gold into the diverse profusion of green.

I was in Pencelli Forest, searching for historic ghosts, following in the footsteps of the great men and commoners of the past who lived, worked and loved this north-west corner of Dyfed, called Demetia by the Romans, and later, in the Middle Ages, Pen-fro, now Pembrokeshire.

Breaking into a shallow clearing I faced a steep incline that, not many years ago, I would have taken in my stride with a loaded rucksack on my back; but now approaching my middle seventies, I was forced to change into low gear. With the aid of my thumbstick – one of my old faithfuls – I eventually reached the top.

Nothing stirred the silent air nor broke the stillness. Aeons past, no doubt, some primitive hunter of wild pig rested on this very spot, his watchful eyes on the small cwm below, searching for his evening meal. Perhaps some lonely Roman soldier, Norman knight or Welsh prince, sat dreaming of home, a well-laden table and a bountiful supply of wine.

Below me spread the forest, broken only by open spaces that

caught the light of the sun. Pursuing a downhill course I picked up a path that, I judged, would bring me to the Nant Duad, the stream that enters the forest from the North.

The trees thinned. Ahead I saw a patch of sunlight, and there came to my ears the soft murmur of water.

The Duad sparkled, gurgling merrily as it flowed southwards to join its big brother, the Nevern. On low briars blackberries drank of the cool, clear water. Memories stirred . . . Many years ago, in this paradisical spot, we lit our camp fire and prepared our evening meal . . . As it was then, it is now.

Breathing the elixir of life exuded by the rich verdure, I pressed on, keeping the creepers and undergrowth at bay with my thumbstick. I have seen hikers with hands in pockets or thumbs in belt, and I have wondered how they maintain a rhythm of pace and balance. Never have I wandered the countryside without my old faithful.

Country Quest (1992)

'Four Schoolmistresses'

The authorship of the short book from which the following item is extracted is anonymous but one imagines that the schoolmistresses concerned could well have been refined spinsters, heavily over-dressed in Victorian Summer clothes, and, perhaps, conversing on the latest sensational novel of the season as they walked their chosen routes.

At the end of this account of our decidedly successful tramp through north Wales, it may not be out of place to mention some of the conclusions to which we have come, and the experience we have gained.

1. We have all improved in health, and three of our number have increased in weight.

2. We have come home with our geographical knowledge widened, and our minds stored with memories of beautiful scenery.

3. We have had a seventeen days' holiday for less than £4 10s. each, and withal have done nothing that people in ordinary health, with sufficient common sense, a small bump of locality, a good map, and their 'weather-eye' open, cannot easily accomplish, even in

doubtful weather; for it is the opinion of some at least of our party that Wales looks best in a rainy season, if it does not rain every day.

The *distances* done by us were as a rule very moderate. The following list may be interesting:

1st day	6 miles	
2nd "	11 "	
3rd "	13 "	
4th "	12 "	
5th "	7½ "	With hard climbing
6th "	6 "	
7th "	13½ "	8 inches rain
8th "	6 "	
9th "	9 "	including Moel Hebog
10th "	16 "	including Snowdon
11th "	21 "	6 too many
12th "	6 "	
13th "	17 "	including Cader Idris
14th "	8 "	
15th "	2 "	
16th "	18½ "	9½ in steady rain and *mud*
17th "	2 "	
making a total of	174½ miles	

We have given all the distances actually walked, though it will be seen that on Sundays and other restdays, they consisted rather of short strolls than real walks.

An *analysis* of our expenditure may also be of use.

	£	s	d
Railway fares for four (including two short journeys)	3	16	9½
Lodgings for 17 nights for four	4	15	9
Food for 17 days	7	9	9
Drives and admission to places of interest	1	7	2½
Miscellaneous expenses		4	0
	£17	13	6

Through North Wales with a Knapsack (1890)

Michael Farraday
(1791-1867)

'Every time we switch on the light, or the radio or television, or summon the aid of a computer we should remember Michael Farraday. He is not only not dead, but is constantly at our elbow.'

So ran an editorial in 'The Guardian' on the 27th August, 1967, the centenary of this great scientists death. To him we owe the discovery of electrical power, and so, in a very important sense, he was a key figure in the development of the world as we know it today.

When a young man he visited Wales and wrote of his impressions of the country and its people.

Monday Morning, July 26th, 1819:
I was so tired last night that instead of writing I took to my bed. I have an excuse for this in not having slept well the night before at Machynlleth. But I am now in excellent plight having a little time before me you shall hear what I have to say of the mountains. We breakfasted at Machynlleth and about quarter past eight found ourselves on the road in the direction of Cader Idris. The vale of the river Dyfi in which Machynlleth stands is very fine in its scenery and forms not only on the side by which we descended but throughout and particularly at that part which we latterly crossed. The river Dovey runs along its northern side, a beautiful stream as clear as air and with a light tint of blue which mountain streams generally possess. We saw the trout sparking along beneath its surface, indeed nothing could be hidden by its pellucid current. Cattle resorted to it for its refreshing assistance and collecting in groups stood in its waters ruminating.

We soon left the vale and passed up into the hollows between the hills. Everything here was delightful, well wooded, well watered and Cader Idris every now and then peeping over at us. The people we met were all cleaned up in their best for the Sunday. Most were either in Church or going to it for the Welch are very religious in their habits and have many sects among them. The principal portion are I believe Methodists. There is a considerable number of the established Church and the rest are Unitarians, Quakers, Jumpers, etc. I have before mentioned the man who conducted us to some of the falls at Neath and who, an Unitarian combined in himself the threefold office of preacher, weaver and guide.

July 25, 1819:
The road wound in a very amusing manner into the mountain generally following the course of a fine blue stream which came from the place we were going to. The groups of people were very different as ornaments on the landscape to any exhibited on common days. They had their shoes and stockings on and their kerchiefs were properly adjusted. They generally appeared in twos or threes with their books and staff. An old man would walk before with a young one behind reading. Now and then a little girl would trot on our way to the school learning her task. In one place where the scenery was very wild and romantic a river being on our left at the bottom of a deep woody dell, high hills on our right and Cader Idris before us, we were suddenly arrested by melody, and stopped to enjoy sounds which added inexpressible interest to the scene. They came from a small simple building with plain latch doors and were those of children amongst which that of a man was evident. The melody was slow and plaintive and came over the ear in full stream undisturbed by any other sound save now and then the murmur of the river beneath at time heightened into a roar by the wind but it added to the effect never disturbing only varying. The building appeared to be a school and the children were chanting a Welch psalm. I never heard sounds that charmed me as these did. Never did music give me such pleasure before. I regretted the moment when they ceased to vibrate and left us to sink down into common life again. But all pleasures are fleeting and this was amongst the most so that I ever possessed.

Michael Farraday in Wales, edited by Dafydd Tomos

Don Frampton

Don Frampton lives in Devon and this account of walking in the border region appears here for the first time.

Crickhowell is a pleasant small mid-Wales town, popular with walkers and it's easy to see why, as the hills all around offer some spectacular walks. Crickhowell stretches along the north east side of the river Usk and on the south western slopes of the mass of the

Black Mountains. The other side of the Usk Valley reaches up to the summit of Llangatwg and on into the Brecon Beacons. To appreciate the way nature sculptured the Usk Valley we shall climb to the top of Table Mountain. From there we should see the whole panorama of the river Usk and the Usk Valley as it drifts slowly south and east into Monmouthshire.

For the afternoon stroll to Table Mountain we start virtually from the pub front door and turn up a side street which quickly takes us up and out of the small town. Suddenly we realise we are actually walking, feeling the conscious effort of pushing oneself and a light rucksack up a hill.

If you are away from walking for some time, maybe ten to fourteen days, then it's a little bit like starting all over again. It is rather a nice feeling, getting back into one's stride.

We soon leave the quiet country lane and climb over a stile and onto grass, another nice feeling. The climb is gentle just enough of an effort for a group of six people, whose combined ages touch 350 years, to feel the benefit. And so up we gently climb the easy grass slopes, turning frequently to admire what the Usk Valley is now laying out for us in an ever increasing panorama as we gain height. It's early January and we have struck it rich with the weather, ice blue skies and just too cold for even a smudge of cloud in the crystal clear air. Every feature of the valley stands in perfect focus. It's just grand to be out.

Table Mountain must have been climbed by many thousands yet for us first timers she has a wicked little surprise for us. The slope gradually gets steeper until we reach a broad track, wide enough for a four wheel drive, which seems to corkscrew around and up the mountain. We follow this for a short distance and then climb off it and sharply up no more than a thirty foot climb to the flat summit. And as your head peaks over the ridge it hits you. Here a thousand howling banshees are having a permanent disco; it's called wind, wind at a thousand miles an hour and we are not ready for it; it tears at every atom of solid material as if desperate to throw everyone and everything back over the ridge, wind to sweep the table top perfectly clean. We cling on and lean into it at 45 degrees. For me, wearing hearing aids, the noise is just unbelievable but when one turns them off, they become like ear muffs and suddenly the wind is reduced to a cringing whine. We take a severe buffeting as we stagger across the flat table; it's a little bit like being on the tube in the rush hour, that feeling of not quite being in charge of one's own destination.

Some kind souls had constructed a wind break out of the large rocks which offered some shelter from the wind so here we sit drinking flask tea and eating cake, grinning at each other in the sheer fun and pleasure of being here, totally away from anyone else just listening to and feeling the planet.

Nature has her way and we are shooed off the table and back to the peace and quiet of the leeside slopes. The walk down is a pleasant amble, we forget the strict path and let our feet follow what feels like the right way and half an hour or so later we are back amongst the neat rowed houses and a short walk takes us back to base, a bath and a book for an hour or so before dinner.

Morning sees us up bright and early. A brief perambulation around town and we are ready for the short meandering drive through narrow country lanes, climbing slightly up the vale of Ewyas along the side of the Afon Honddu to the car park at Abbey Farm.

The walk starts from a path running up the side of Abbey Farm, most of which has been built from the stone of the old ruined abbey which was built in about 1107 by William De Lacy who was the brother of the then Bishop of Salisbury. The farm and the remains of the old ruined abbey sit side by side on the west facing slope of the valley. They look very comfortable, as though they have always been there. The Abbey and therefore the farm, were built of the local stone so are very much part of the landscape – as though little pieces have been borrowed from nature and simply re-arranged a little distance from where nature originally placed them.

The question always comes to mind. Why did the monks leave after such hard work? The story goes they were not all that welcomed by the local people despite their attempts to make beer and sell to the surrounding peasants. Maybe it's all summed up with the comment at the time by the brethren, 'Why should we stay here and sing to the wolves?' Anyway, after a mere thirty year of occupancy they packed their bags and left for Gloucester.

We walked up a well worn track known as Rhiw Cwrw or Beer Track as it was used by the monks of the Abbey to carry their beer between Lanthony and Longtown on the eastern side of the ridge. It's a good climb first across fields and then into the bracken and up a steep rising slope to the top of the ridge where we turn right on to a section of Offa's Dyke. For the benefit of those not familiar with Offa I can tell you that he was the king of Mercia. The Dyke can still be seen, stretching for miles across the Welsh countryside and, in some instances through the centre of towns. Now it forms one of the most pleasant national footpaths in Britain. I know Offa's Dyke quite well because with a few friends we have walked maybe two-thirds of it starting from the North coast of Wales thus far have reached the town of Hay on Wye, known as the town of books. It's been a very slow walk, we started it about 25 years ago and we hope to finish it before another 25 years pass us by.

From the top of the ridge the view back down the valley and across to the far Western ridge is breathtaking, the pattern of fields edged by the intricate fretted outline of winter's undressed trees, the winter green of the fields edged again on the upper slopes by the dull dead brown of bracken. It is winter's sun at its very best. Turning around, the view to the east and south extends deep into Shropshire and the famous mound of Long Mynd and then south and west across the wandering misty ridges of the Brecon Beacons. To the far East the view stretches to the shadowy outlines of the Malvern Hills, which border Shropshire and Worcestershire.

The walk along the ridge is all too short. It is one of those very special January days when the cold crisp air reaches up to the purest of blue skies, paling at the horizon but imperceptibly changing its colour until it reaches over one's head with an ever increasing density of colour; stretching one's neck to look straight up you can let your eyes touch that wonderful, limitless dark blue of eternity. Here, where the hillsides and valleys sing out silently one can realise why so many of England's great composers, Elgar, Vaughan Williams, Butterworth all came here to Wales, and were inspired.

To stand here with a contoured walking map in one's hand one can transfer the swirling mass of rings which marks the heights and gradients of hills and valleys from the map onto the countryside before you and realise you are looking at the fingerprints of nature herself upon the surface of the land.

The eastern side of the ridge is the lee side, sheltering us from the strong cold wind blowing up the Olthon valley and pushing hard against the western slopes. This is hang gliding country and maybe a dozen of these fixed wing bees are hovering off the steep slopes, moving up and down the ridge seeking upward current to give them height. To venture out of the shelter of the lee to the ridge edge is to risk losing one's head gear and being chilled to the bone in minutes, so we take a sheltered lunch before starting the descent.

The way is down, past Pentwyn Hill fort, an Iron Age construction still quite sharp in outline, and on to a rough track leading to a narrow road which takes us to the bottom of the valley. Here we recognise the Queen's Head pub and the road which we had taken up to the car park, but for us the walk is not yet over. We have covered more than half our twelve mile stroll but there are maybe four or five still in front of us.

The guide book describes this road as a seemingly endlessly upward journey. It is. It twists and turns, at each bend one breathes to oneself that this must be the last; it just must run out of upwardness, but it doesn't. It just seems to go on and on upward and upward. The top is marked by another clearly defined Iron Age fort —Gaer Hill. Those iron age folk had a lot of basic cunning, they just knew any invading force would have been absolutely powfagged by the time they got to the top of the hill and it would have been a case of simply banging them on the head with your iron age hammer.

Finally, we break out onto the open moorland and again the heavens open with the late afternoon wall to wall sky. You can't get tired when walking in scenery like this; it's the exhilaration of the mid afternoon glow. Down in the valley to the right we can again see the ruins of the abbey and the farm which abuts it and let the eyes wander effortlessly across the slope we toiled up this morning. To the left towards the now early setting sun The Darren, a red sandstone cliff, glows, the very earth has a rosy healthy look about it.

We still have about a three mile walk but it is level and firm underfoot so we can relax after the hill climb and enjoy this. The path takes us to a small rough stone unmarked memorial known as the Dialgarreg or the stone of revenge. It marks the spot where in 1135 one Richard De Clare, a Norman knight, met his come-uppance at the hands of a bunch of the local lads led by one Morgan Ap Owen. At Bal Mawr, a height of 1800 feet, the sun has virtually set and the day is turning cold and so at the monument of

Garn Wen – a well cared for circular cairn – we turn east and start our last descent into the Ewyas valley to complete our day's journey.

Sunday, and the weather is holding good, it promises clear skies and a prosperous voyage if you can describe a walk up the Sugar Loaf as a voyage. Today is but a short though quite strenuous walk, the climb to the top of The Sugar Loaf will give us an ascent of some 1300 feet, the last three to four hundred feet being quite steep.

The hill stands in almost splendid isolation from the rest of the area. One sees it well before we stop to boot up and start the walk. It looks a nice little hill but then as we get closer it becomes quite a big hill, a very big hill, and there is a good mile of gradually increasing incline before we get to the base and look up. It's huge and we can see people the size of ants attacking it from all directions some on the way up others in retreat. Why is it that the urge to get to the top is so strong? Some sense of achievement?

The wind at the top does its very best to push us off and back down into the valley. But again that wonderful feeling of space and distance, of quiet, of almost being overawed; a genuine feeling of loving it and wanting to care for all one sees as it's all so precious. To walk lightly. Not to break it, because we want to come back and see it all over again.

Peter Finch

As well as being an extremely popular poet Peter Finch is also the director of the Academi, the agency in Wales which is responsible for the promotion of literature.

Watkin Path

up the crowded slog
which four-foot fat
Manon did two years back so
I daren't complain a gent in
tweeds bravely pulling on a
woodbine stopped on the
zig-zags sun no rock

painted Bashô haiku but
the train on Crib y Ddysgl
out of Dali the summit
clog gross llanbuggery white
heeled handbag the way
off retaining grace is Sir Edward
Watkin's 1890 vertical heartstop
descended jellyleg vertigo
and blind then the long miles to
Gladstone's great ice-polished
slab where he once addressed the
people of Eryri on justice and I
lie for half an hour to see if
the shaking stops sky still there
dry blue and most of it still up

Thomas Firbank
(1910-2001)

One of the enduring bestsellers in Wales within the last fifty years has been I
Bought a Mountain, *an account of Firbank's experiences as a sheep farmer in
Snowdonia in the nineteen thirties. Among his other books was* A Country of
Memorable Honour. *In it he describes in lively detail a journey on foot from
Llangollen to Cardiff. It ranks with* Wild Wales *in the Welsh travel genre.
Here we find him at the start of his walk.*

I crossed the border on foot. The little town which I reached on the
mid-February morning lay in the cupped palm of the hills, through
whose deep-cleft lifeline flowed a swift river. The sun was above
the mountains and the pale winter rays struck cold light from the
snow crystals which covered the bridge on which I paused. I stood
in an embrasure above one of the abutments and looked up-river
deeper into the strange country. The hills encircled the town with
an unbroken rim, white on the skyline, but tree-clothed lower
down, each branch of the topmost rows of larches fretted clear
against the snow.

The river slid by quickly, blue-black when it lingered in the
deeper pools, lathered with cold sweat when it leaped down the
rapids. Just above the bridge the water divided to pass a flat rock

which lay in its course like a stranded whale. Passers-by gave each other good morning and remarked on the weather in their melodious foreign tongue, for at this season there were no visitors or sightseers, and the place had lost the self-consciousness of the tourist centre.

A Country of Memorable Honour (1953)

Catherine Fisher

Hikers

They crowd the door of the guest-house,
eyes on the sky; the white summits;
hooded, file through the birds' welcome,
the clutter of shops,
the opening shutters,
straight to the stark ridges of the hills.

None of them can explain it, the urgency,
the rhythm of striding
releasing the mind like meditation;
the rosary of the road.
Nothing, after hours, but sky,
a snatch of conversation,
a poem's line
like a mantra on hills and fells.

Monks and mendicants, I have worn their coat,
desired their oblivion, the trudging
from somewhere to nowhere;
felt the summit's elation,
the dreadful descent;
prophets returning with the Law
that is smashed in the valley.

Raymond Garlick

Raymond Garlick has played an enormously important role in the development of Welsh poetry in English within the last fifty years through his own poetic output, his work as an anthologist and as a critic.

Winter Walk

The squealing snow
beneath my tread
perhaps woke the lurking
words in my head:

'Sometimes, after weeks
of implacable snow,
one has been seen.
Better not go.

too deep in the forest
in such a year:
hunger will run them
across the frontier.'

On the snow's white page
the textbook signs
slunk down the dazzle
between the pines –

the narrow inscription
of single dints,
each pad placed
in the other's prints,

a couple of hand-lengths
between each set.
The noiseless forest
spread out its net

of chiaroscuro –
like hyacinth
beneath the branches;
a labyrinth

of light on the paths,
a polar fur,
vividly slashing
the blue shade's blur.

Returning homewards,
threading the hours
and kilometres
back to the house,

each bush had eyes,
unseen but felt,
each crouching log
a grey-black pelt.

Richard George

Map-reading the Marches

These names meant something long ago,
Mountain, farmstead, church:
But centuries and English tongues
Have weathered Welsh to sound and shape,
Skyborry, Knucklas,
Craggy and distinctive as each incline.

Between these names the land unfolds
By contour, spot-height, trig point;
Station halt, Llanbister Road,
Inches from its village.
It puts us in our place,
Around each step a radius; solitude.

But some things maps don't show you.
Under Spoad's four hundred metre hog's back
Newcastle-on-Clun, in blue,
Play Knucklas on a Sunday
To an audience of black-faced sheep
Browsing each touch-line.

William Gilpin
(1724-1802)

Gilpin's 'Observations on the River Wye' is acknowledged as the most influential work of the picturesque and has been described as 'the aethetic bible of a new cult'. He believed that the beauty to be found in a landscape could be judged by its suitability to an artist's work.

We now began to ascend its steeps; but before we had risen too high, we turned round to take a retrospect of all the rich scenes together, which we had left behind. It was a noble view; distance melting into distance; till the whole was closed by a semi-circle of azure sky, which absorbed them.

Still ascending the spiral road round the shaggy side of the mountain, we arrived at what is called its *gate*. Here all ideas of cultivation ceased. That was not deplorable: but with it our turnpike-road ceased also; which was finished, on this side, no farther than the *mountain-gate*. We had gotten a guide however to conduct us over the pathless desart. But it being too steep and rugged to ascend on wheels, we were obliged to lighten our carriage, and ascend on foot.

In the midst of our labour, our guide called out, that he saw a storm driving towards us, along the tops of the mountains; a circumstance indeed, which in these hilly countries cannot often be avoided. We asked him, How far it was off? He answered, Ten minutes. In less time, sky, mountains and vallies were all wrapt in one cloud of obscurity.

Our recompense consisted in following with our eye the rear of the storm; observing, through its broken skirts, a thousand beautiful effects, and half-formed images, which were continually opening, lost, and varying; till the sun breaking out, the whole resplendent landscape appeared again, with double radiance, under the leaden gloom of the retiring tempest.

Observations on the River Wye,
and several parts of south Wales (1782)

George Gissing
(1857-1903)

One of the most important English novelists of his day, Gissing's work tended to be neglected in the half century which followed.
Although he wrote much fiction with London settings, in The Whirlpool *a part of the story takes the characters to Llŷn.*
Gwyn Neale has devoted an interesting book to the author's associations with north Wales, All the Days Were Glorious.

The pedestrians took their way along a winding road, between boulder walls thick-set with the new leaves of pennywort; then crossed the one long street of the town (better named a village), passing the fountain, overbuilt with lichened stone, where women and children filled their cans with sweet water, sparkling in the golden light. Rolfe now and then received a respectful greeting. He had wished to speak Welsh, but soon abandoned the endeavour. He liked to hear it, especially on the lips of children at their play. An old, old language, symbol of the vitality of a race; sounding on those young lips as in the time when his own English, composite, hybrid, had not yet begun to shape itself.

Beyond the street and a row of cottages, they began to climb; at first a gentle ascent, on either hand high hedges of flowering blackthorn, banks strewn with primroses and violets, and starred with the white stitchwort; great leaves of foxglove giving promise for future days. The air was bland, yet exquisitely fresh; scented from innumerable sources in field and heath and wood. When the lane gave upon open ground, they made a pause to look back. Beneath them lay the little grey town, and beyond it the grassy cliffs, curving about a blue bay. Near by rose the craggy slopes of a bare hill, and beyond it, a few miles to the north, two lofty peaks, wreathed against the cloudless heaven with rosy mist.

'Sure it won't be too much for you?' said Harvey looking upwards to the wooded height.

'I feel equal to anything,' answered his companion brightly.

'This air has given me new life.'

There was a faint colour on her cheeks, and for the first time Harvey caught an expression which reminded him of the face he had known years ago, when Mrs Abbott looked upon life much as Alma did now.

They entered upon a rising heath, green with mosses where the moisture of a hidden stream drew downwards, brown with dead bracken on dry slopes. Just above was a great thicket of flowering gorse; a blaze of colour, pure, aerial, as that of the sky which illumined it. Through this they made their way, then dropped into a green nook of pasture, among sheep that raised their heads distrustfully, and loud-bleating lambs, each running to its mother.

'If you can scale this wall, it will save us a quarter of an hour.'

'If you can, I can.' was the laughing reply.

Protruding boulders made it an easy clamber. They were then at the base of Carn Bodvean, and before them rose steep mountain glades. Mrs Abbott gazed upwards with unspoken delight.

'There are no paths,' said Harvey. 'It's honest woodland. Some day it will be laid out with roads and iron benches, with finger-posts, "To the summit".'

'You think so?'

'Why, of course. It's the destiny of every beautiful spot in Britain. There'll be a pier down yonder, and a switchback railway, and leagues of lodging-houses, and brass bands.'

'Let us hope we shall be dead.'

The Whirlpool (1897)

Nathaniel Hawthorne
(1804-1864)

Hawthorne was for one period of his life, the American consul in Liverpool. He wrote an extensive journal recording his impressions of people and places which he visited during his seemingly long periods of leisure. These did not appear in print until after his death.

The following item written in 1853 concerns a walk which he took in the flat landscape between Rhuddlan and Rhyl, which happens to be one which I often follow myself.

. . . we set out to walk along the embankment, although the sky looked very threatening. The wind, however, was so strong, and had such a full sweep at us on the top of the bank, that we decided on taking a path that led from it across the moor. But we soon had cause to repent of this; for, which way so ever we turned, we found ourselves cut off by a ditch or a little stream; so that here we were, fairly astray on Rhyddlan moor, the old battle-field of the Saxons and Britons, and across which, I suppose, the fiddlers and mountebanks had marched to the relief of the Earl of Chester. Anon, too, it began to shower; and it was only after various leaps and scramblings that we made our way, to a large farm-house, and took shelter under a cart-shed. The back of the house to which we gained access was very dirty and ill kept; some dirty children peeped at us as we approached, and nobody had the civility to ask us in; so we took advantage of the first cessation of the shower to resume our way. We were shortly overtaken by a very intelligent-looking and civil man, who seemed to have come from Rhyddlan, and, said he was going to Rhyl. We followed his guidance over stiles and along hedge-row paths which we never could have threaded rightly by ourselves.

By-and-by our kind guide had to stop at an intermediate farm, but he gave us full directions how to proceed, and we went on till it began to shower again pretty briskly, and we took refuge in a little bit of old stone cottage, which, small as it was, had a greater antiquity than any mansion in America. The door was open, and as we approached, we saw several children gazing at us; and their mother, a pleasant-looking woman, who seemed rather astounded at the visit that was about to befall her, tried to draw a tattered curtain over part of her interior, which she fancied even less fit to be seen than the rest. To say the truth, the house was not at all better than a pigsty; and while we sat there, a pig came familiarly to the door, thrust in his snout, and seemed surprised that he should be driven away, instead of being admitted as one of the family. The floor was of brick; there was no ceiling, but only the peaked gable overhead. The room was kitchen, parlour, and I suppose, bedroom for the whole family; at all events, there was only the tattered curtain between us and the sleeping accommodations. The good woman either could not or would not speak a word of English, only laughing when S. said, 'Dim Sassenach', but she was kind and hospitable, and found a chair for each of us. She had been making some bread, and the dough was on the dresser. Life with these people is reduced to its simplest elements. It is only a pity that they cannot or do not choose to keep themselves cleaner. Poverty, except in cities, need not be squalid. When the shower abated a little, we gave all the pennies we had to the children, and set forth again.

Passages from the English Notebooks (1870)

William Hazlitt
(1778-1830)

This supreme critic and essayist spent much of his childhood close to the Welsh border, at Wem in Shropshire. His output of writing was prolific and he believed that 'genuine criticism should reflect the colour, the light and shade, and body of a work'.

One of his most memorable essays is On Going a Journey *from which this passage is taken.*

It was on the 10th of April 1790 that I sat down to a volume of the 'New Eloise', at the inn at Llangollen, over a bottle of sherry and a cold chicken. The letter I chose was that in which St Preux describes his feelings as he first caught a glimpse from the heights of the Jura of the Pays de Vaud, which I had brought with me as a *bon bouche* to crown the evening with. It was my birthday, and I had for the first time come from a place in the neighbourhood to visit this delightful spot. The road to Llangollen turns off between Chirk and Wrexham; and on passing a certain point you come all at once upon the valley, which opens like an amphitheatre, broad, barren hills rising in majestic state on either side, with 'green upland swells that echo to the bleat of flocks' below, and the river Dee babbling over its stony bed in the midst of them. The valley at this time 'glittered green with sunny showers', and a budding ash-tree dipped its tender branches in the chiding stream. How proud, how glad I was to walk along the highroad that overlooks the delicious prospect, repeating the lines which I have just quoted from Mr Coleridge's poems! But besides the prospect which opened beneath my feet, another also opened to my inward sight, a heavenly vision, on which were written, in letters large as Hope could make them, these four words, LIBERTY, GENIUS, LOVE, VIRTUE, which have since faded into the light of common day, or mock my idle gaze.

The beautiful is vanished and returns not.

Still, I would return some time or other to this enchanted spot, but I would return to it alone. What other self could I find to share that influx of thoughts, of regret, and delight, the fragments of which I could hardly conjure up to myself, so much have they been broken and defaced? I could stand on some tall rock, and overlook the precipice of years that separates me from what I then was. I was at that time going shortly to visit the poet whom I have above named. Where is he now? Not only I myself have changed; the world, which was then new to me, has become old and incorrigible. Yet will I turn to thee in thought, O sylvan Dee, in joy, in youth and gladness as thou then wert; and thou shalt always be to me the river of Paradise, where I will drink of the waters of life freely!

On Going a Journey

John Hillaby

Yorkshire born John Hillaby was an inveterate walker, and his travels took him across the length and breadth of Britain, through Europe, from the North Sea to the Mediterranean, and across regions of Canada and tropical Africa.

Apart from brief excursions into Snowdonia, the forests of Montgomeryshire and a walk down Offa's Dyke, that boundary laid down by the king of the Mercians, I know little about what most people associate with Wales. The TV people suggested I might do something in the footsteps of George Borrow, but after plodding from Chester towards Anglesey with a copy of his *Wild Wales* in my pocket, I gave up, impressed only by the wild traffic. The following year we nearly bought a large plot of land cheaply in central Wales, but found the natives of Machynlleth nearly as difficult to get on with as it is to pronounce the name of their attractive little town.

Journey Through Love (1976)

Despite thick, mature woods and rolling downland, Radnorshire is a strangely lonely, nobody-about place, the most sparsely populated county in England and Wales. The inhabitants are not at all sure, most of them, whether they are English or Welsh and the majority, fortunately, don't seem to care. At the last count, only a handful of families said they preferred to speak Welsh. Most of the people you meet know only a few words related to place-names, such as *Gil-fach*, the little retreat, *Fron-las*, the green bank, *Pen-y-bont*, the head of the bridge and *Sais*, which is Englishman.

What catches the ear is not so much the extraordinarily variable accent, as the inversions and idioms which come through from the Welsh. They say 'Good evening' in the afternoon. They tend to speak demonstratively: 'Stay you there now and I'll ask him.' Pronouns are tossed about indiscriminately. 'So him told I you was looking for Herrock.' A Radnorshire tombstone is inscribed:

His as was has gone from we;
Us as is must go to he.

Weather is usually the first topic of conversation and fields are sometimes referred to as 'she'. 'She's not bearing well now,' they say. 'Not with that fancy dressing stuff.'

Journey through Britain (1968)

Jeremy Hooker

Walking the Cliff Path

1.
As we climb, head and lungs clear,
The sky lifts, the blue-grey sea
Reflects a watery sun.

From cliffs with gulls below
The eye falls south, over
Arched, long-necked
Headlands, and returns
In a slow flight inland
From islands of volcanic rock.

68

Then the path descends
Into a hollow of gorse
And stonechats; heat brings out
The flies that love us; we clump
With skewed feet over stones.

2.
Ar Carregwastad Point
We rest.
The 'last invasion'
Ended here, in drunkenness
And pillage.

Why here? Pen Caer
Was its own protector.
Still only the sea wastes it,
And the acid lichen.

If I could paint
I would use its colours
On a surface of stone.

Blue-grey for the sea.
Green and brown earth colours.
Yellow for tormentil.
Red for the brick defences
Of a later war.

For the billy goat
That lives there,
Wagging his beard,
The colour of rock itself.

3.
Some stones I return to
For those they commemorate;
To others for themselves.

We cannot read this one
To Dewi Emrys.

Your Welsh soon falters.
I stand monoglot before it.

And because we cannot read it,
We turn aside, listening
To a yellowhammer repeating
Its dry whistle on a thorn.

It is like a bird practising
To sing; but this is its song,
Ending always with a *Tzee*.

from *Pembrokeshire Journey*

Clyde Holmes

Clyde Holmes is both a poet and an impressive landscape painter. He lives in a remote cottage in Snowdonia.

Track
Carnedd y Filiast, Cwm Hesgin

I walk all day.
Mountains still before me,
same colours near and far.
Chestnut-tinged blobs of peat,
setting sun rises as I climb,
rays of amber and grub-grey.
Boulders break out of the ground
relieved of earth's burden.
Peaks shape haze,
change with every stride.
In the valley
distant gloom becomes
space within a vessel.
The track loses itself . . .
on my shadow, dust settles.

Winter Time

Llangower

We walk through the village;
footfalls fossilise in snow
with hushed clamour of a dream.

We pass the churchyard.
The still bell watches over graves,
preserves our silence.

Guy Fawkes' Night

for John Davies

We climbed above Prestatyn
and paused for breath,
took in a full tide of townlights.
Fireworks were shelling
over flame-matted mounds,
colours streaked and dripped.

On the sky's blacked-out canvas
a gibbous moon restored woods'
parting by Offa's Dyke –
openly showed us
the border's old scar.

Gerard Manley Hopkins
(1844-1889)

Hopkins spent the period from 1874 to 1877 undergoing his training for the Jesuit priesthood at St Beuno's College, near St Asaph. Although the strict order of which he was a member did not encourage the writing of poetry, this did not stop Hopkins from writing some of his best remembered work.

He walked extensively in the Vale of Clwyd and Hurrahing in Harvest *was, in his own words, 'the outcome of half an hour of extreme enthusiasm as I walked home alone one day from fishing in the Elwy'.*

Hurrahing in Harvest

Summer ends now; now, barbarous in beauty, the stooks rise
Around; up above, what wind-walks! what lovely behaviour
Of silk-sack clouds! has wilder, wilful-wavier
Meal-drift moulded ever and melted across skies?

I walk, I lift up, I lift up heart, eyes,
Down all that glory in the heavens to glean our Saviour;
And, eyes, heart, what looks, what lips yet gave you a
Rapturous love's greeting of realer, of rounder replies?

And the azurous hung hills are his world-wielding shoulder
Majestic – as a stallion stalwart, very-violet-sweet! –
These things, these things were here and but the beholder
Wanting; which two when they once meet,
The heart rears wings bold and bolder
And hurls for him, O half hurls earth for him off under his feet.

A party of us set out for Moel Fammau, the highest of the hills
bounding the valley and distant as the crow flies about nine miles.
There stands on it what remains of the Jubilee Tower erected in
honour of George III's 50th year of royalty, an ugly and trumpery
construction, make-believe-massive but so frail that it was blown
over by the gale that wrecked the Royal Charter, and it cumbers
the hilltop and interrupts the view. As we walked along the hills
towards it the valley looked more charming and touching than
ever: in its way there can hardly be in the world anything to beat
the Vale of Clwyd. The day was then threatening and clouded, the
sea and distant hills brimmed with purple, clouds trailing low, the
landscape clear but sober, the valley though so verdant appeared
of a pale blush-colour from the many red sandstone fresh-
ploughed fields. Clarke and I made one of the only two couples
that reached Moel Fammau. When we had come down into the
valley the day became very beautiful.

From his Journal

Bitter north wind, hail and sleet. On the hills snow lying and the mountains covered from head to foot. But they could scarcely be seen till next day, a Blandyke, which was fine and clear. I went with Mr Hughes up Moel y Parc, from the top of which we had a noble view, but the wind was very sharp. Snowdon and all the range reminded me of the Alps: they looked like a stack of rugged white flint, specked and streaked with black, in many places chiselled and channelled. Home by Caerwys wood, where we saw two beautiful swans, as white as they should be, restlessly steering and 'canting' in the water and following us along the shore: one of them several times, as if for vexation, caught and gnawed at the stone quay of the sluice close under me.

From a letter to his mother

Hopkins had visited Wales prior to his period at St Beunos. In the following journal extract we find him in the Wye valley.

Smart showers in morning with bright between; this cleared till it was very fine, with flying clouds casting shadows on the Wye hills. Fine sunset. – Tintern to Ross by Monmouth.

The afternoon way we much enjoyed, in especial we turned down a grass lane to reach the river at the ferry. It was steep down at first and I remember blue sprays of wych-elm or hazel against the sunlight green further on. Then the fields rose high on each side, one crowned with beautiful trees (there was particularly an ash with you could not tell how many contradictory supple curvings in the boughs), and then orchards, of which this country is full; on the other, with a narrow plot of orchard in which sheep grazed between the rise and the lane, was Goderich castle of red sandstone on the height. Close by the river was a fine oak with long lunging boughs. The country full of fine trees, especially oaks, and is, like Devonshire, on red soil. We crossed the river whirling down with a swollen stream, and then by lanes to Ross.

From his Journal (1866)

Joseph Hucks
(1772-1800)

Hucks was a Cambridge undergraduate when he undertook a walking tour of north Wales in 1795. His companion was Samuel Taylor Coleridge. Quite apart from anything else Hucks offers us some insight into the personality of one of the greatest figures of the English Romantic Movement.

See Samuel Taylor Coleridge page 35

It was with much difficulty we found our way to Harlech. We made some enquiries at a small village, but in vain; for though we addressed ourselves to many, we could by no means make them understand us; all we received in return was a stare, immediately followed by a grin, and concluded with a 'tin sarcenick', which signifies 'no Saxon'. We were obliged therefore to rely upon chance for our guide, which did not however upon this occasion befriend us; for, instead of keeping to the right upon the hills, we pursued the left path, that brought us into an extensive vale, or marsh, where, at the distance of about five miles, we first perceived the objects we were in pursuit of (viz.) the town and castle of Harlech. After some considerable exertions, we were obliged to abandon this valley, because it was so swampy, and so much intersected by ditches and drains, that it would have been, if not impracticable, at least extremely uncomfortable and difficult to proceed. With great fatigue and perseverance, we climbed up the almost perpendicular, and craggy sides of the mountain, which bounded that part of the vale, where we were reduced to the above perplexity, and at length reached Harlech; for the first time heartily fatigued.

The country people have no idea that a stranger can be ignorant of their roads; we have not infrequently asked the way, and received for answer, 'That it was as straight as we could go': when, in a very few paces, we had been perplexed by two roads, one declining to the right, and the other to the left. Nor have they very much idea of distance; each measuring it by rule of his own judgement and opinion. It is no unusual thing to be told that the distance to such a place may be about five miles 'and a pretty good step': which pretty good step generally proves to be about five miles more.

From Barmouth to Dolegelly we were highly gratified; the road wound along a ridge of rocks, that hang over the Avonvawr, an arm of the sea; which, at full tide, has the appearance of a large lake, surrounded with beautiful woods: The mountains on both sides, but particularly on the opposite shore, were strikingly grand; and above all, Cader Idris reared its head into the clouds, which, together with the sombre aspect of the evening, and the hollow murmurings of the sea gave an awful sublimity to the scene that cannot be described.

Dolegelly is a large and dirty town and we took up our quarters at the Golden Lion, a good hospitable inn; and next morning, after breakfast, procured a guide to conduct us to the top of Cader Idris. We armed him with stores, and warlike preparations of all kinds (to wit): ham, fowl, bread and cheese, and brandy, and began the ascent at nine in the morning, and continued to toil for three hours and a half before we reached the top. But, alas! expectation had again flattered us; for, though it was a most lovely day in the valleys, yet here we could not see.

Joseph Hucks: A Pedestrian Tour through North Wales in a Series of Letters edited by Alun R. Jones and William Tydeman (1979)

Cledwyn Hughes

. . . It is a long pull from Watkin's Farm to the village church, which is set on one of the first foothills of Wales. On sunny summer mornings it is an enjoyable walk to Matins, and under frosty stars on a cold winter's night it can be one of the most rewarding journeys given to any thinking and conscious man; but tonight there was the bitter east wind which had caught me by the Old Clay Pool in the morning. But there were no stars, and the ceiling was of snow clouds; the wind in the bare branches of the trees, and through the high thorn hedges, had all the promise of coming snow or sleet or that icy rain which comes from the east beyond the Wrekin of the Shropshire Plain.

The House in the Cornfield (1957)

R.G. Hughes

This item is extracted from an unpublished document in which the writer records his life as a miner at Point of Ayr colliery in Flintshire.

One thing strikes me very forceably and it is the fact that out of five hundred men employed at the time only one was an Englishman. How cosmopolitan the pit has become since those days! The banksman was an old hand, Joe Luke from Mostyn. Should he be absent his place would be taken by another old gentleman, William Jones, Y Mwynt, as he was known. He walked from Trelogan with his umbrella, starting out at 5 a.m. It was known for some of these old miners who walked from Trelogan, Newmarket, Penyffordd and Ffynnongroew to turn back if they were only half way to the colliery when the starting hooter went they would consider it too late to proceed! It was an understood thing that to arrive in the lamproom after 5.55 a.m. meant no lamp for you, so it was home James!

From his diary (1932)

Wil Ifan
(1882-1968)

Wil Ifan (William Evans) wrote in both Welsh and English and won the Crown at the National Eisteddfod on no less than three occasions. He was Archdruid for three years.

Some of us have arrived at the age when the predominant urge is to recapture rather than to capture. When one morning I set out on a country road, on the border of Carmarthen and Pembroke, I didn't exactly know what I wanted to recapture, but the pining desire was certainly there.

I had known this road, every inch of it, when I was a boy, but though I realised how foolish it was to dream of knowing again the vitality of boyhood I couldn't help hoping that something of the past was still left in the air.

I had to pass the village shop – if you can call four cottages a village, and a few shelves a shop – which that day boasted but two sorts of sweets, and though I came away with samples of both in my pockets neither sort would take me back where I would be. I had hoped that there might have been a bottle of white 'extra-strongs' or pear-shaped 'lemon drops'.

Even with this initial setback I did not lose heart; I still realised that boyhood, if it was to come back at all, would return by way of my mouth, and so I hopefully scanned the hedges.

The quiet but unambiguous taste of whinberries did their best for me as I remembered the high hedge near Moriah on a Sunday morning. In that long ago we were anxious not to empurple our lips as we never felt satisfied that picking the Sunday berries bore the imprimatur of the papal decrees from our 'Big Seat'.

With the help of my umbrella crook I pulled down some over-hanging hazel branches and, though the nuts were far from ripe, the taste, something between that of milk and raw mushrooms, was certainly evocative, and before long the boy that I was looking for seemed to be walking at my side.

It was such a pity that the Ffynnon Wen motor-car, modernity incarnate, came round the corner at that very moment. Dilwyn at the wheel beamed at me as he careered by, blissfully ignorant of the fact that he had driven the little fellow who was with me into the ditch.

Here and There (1953)

Siân James

In a specially written contribution this award winning novelist recalls a favourite walk in West Wales during her childhood and the people who were part of her world at that time.

A track in West Wales leading downhill to the sea, my favourite walk as a child and even now redolent of the past. The hedges are high and full of seaside flowers: little pink thrift, harebell, scabious, sea lavender, ragged robin, speedwell, purple vetch, pennywort, tiny ferns and beautiful nodding grasses; the flora is much as I remember, but today the butterflies are rare and fewer birds sing.

77

As children, my sister and I were always content to spend an hour or more collecting wild flowers – indeed I fear we may have contributed to the depletion of certain species in West Wales – but when Auntie Maggie suggested to our favourite cousin, Dan, that he might like to join us, he looked at her in disbelief and said, 'I beth?' *(What for?)* What was it for? Why couldn't we have simply looked at the flowers and passed by? Oh, but it was an added pleasure to pick and smell and feel them in our hands. I've never been one to kiss joy as it flies, but rather one to hang on to its coat tails as long as I possibly can.

We come to my favourite part, the walk through the woods. Once again I'm full of wonder that a pathway was ever dug out and that it has survived in this steep, rocky place. The trees are very old: mostly oak, ash and beech and grow straight and tall to reach the sun. On a mild summer day, they have an enveloping stillness, a mysterious dream-like quality; they seem the very essence of trees as in certain paintings by Cezanne, and with the green spaces of Rousseau as well. We can hear the stream in the valley, though we can't see it.

Once, my older sister saw a red squirrel in these woods and I, too, very nearly saw it. Once a weasel crossed our path, his tail puffed out with fright and it was pleasant to imagine that a big buck rabbit had seen him off.

Emerging from the woods and seeing the sea in the distance, there would be a great deal of excited chatter. My oldest sister could remember a house that had a notice saying, 'Dŵr berw. Dime.' *(Boiling water. Ha'penny.)* In those days before the war, the nearby farming families brought their huge baskets of food, their table cloths, their second-best tea sets and teapots with them and having boiling water provided at comparatively little expense must have been a godsend.

My mother would tell us about her childhood visits to the sea. Her father was a non-conformist minister and used to spend a month as visiting preacher at a chapel in Porthcawl, so the parents, the maid and eight children would travel there by train every year with one trunk full of socks and stockings and another full of home-made fruit cake. The three girls wore long black stockings every day even on the beach. On the very first day, their father – who was very strict and called 'y cyrnal' *(the colonel)* by his children – would buy them all new plimsoles at threepence a pair to save their school boots and Sunday shoes and woe betide anyone who mislaid or damaged them. In order to rile his father, the middle son, Jack, used to spend much of his time singing and playing tambourine with the Salvation Army Band. On Sundays they only had to go to chapel twice instead of the usual three times. We had heard all these tales many times before – in fact each time we walked to the sea – but we always enjoyed them.

Now I'm telling my children and grandchildren about a wartime world when sweets and chocolates were rationed, bananas unavailable and a custard cream biscuit the very height of luxury. Did we have ice-cream? I don't think so. I remember that when I went to an Urdd camp at Llangrannog when I was eleven or twelve, tomato ketchup was the only thing we succeeded in buying at the village shop without either coupons or points, so that our midnight feasts consisted of dry bread —smuggled out of the canteen under our shirts – spread with this vinegary red sauce. But what did it matter? I'd acquired a boyfriend from Bethesda who'd managed to bring with him a bottle of his baby-sister's orange juice that we sucked from in turn. (Children under three got this thick gooey juice free from the welfare clinic. It was certainly an acquired taste, very sweet but with a sinister undertone. Years later I heard that it was very palatable with gin.)

At the boarding house we stayed at during the war, the greatest treat was the pudding, always stewed apples and custard. Yes, we often had the same at home, but that particular custard must have been made with something really exotic like condensed milk; I can still remember the taste.

When my eldest son was first shown the sea at about a year old, he flung out his arms dramatically as though to encompass it all. I go on to recall all my children at various delightful stages: second son joining every picnicing group hoping for a handout, third son shrieking at the seagulls because, 'they started it', daughter Anna struggling into her swimming costume with extreme modesty, but dragging it off the moment it got the slightest bit wet. I manage to embarrass them all.

And now we've already reached the tea-shop and the grandchildren are clamouring for Theyer's gorgeous ice-cream cornets. (One pound each. When I was a girl, that was a week's rent for a seaside cottage.) And now the last stage, through 'the jungle' down the steps, over the bridge and onto the sandy beach.

And the eternal sea where past and present collide and are
reconciled.

Carol Jones

*In this passage from a prize-winning novel, Carol Jones writes of the area of
mountainous country high above Penmaenmawr.*

Here was a rough lane which led to the mountain proper, through
cliffs and mounds of spoiled granite, the rubbish of a hundred
years. Some, the more recent, weren't even overgrown. All stages
of natural reclamation were evident – couch, bilberry, bramble;
sapling birch, rowan; and everywhere twisted dwarf hawthorns;
gorse, not at present in much flower. The higher one went, the
more entangled the path, until it became nearly impassable. Near
the top, too, each accumulation of stone put one in mind of, and
may have been, an ancient fragment. Tumbled barriers of *chevaux
de frise*, smashed walls which may have formed defences,
massively following the mountain contours.

But I turned on to the shelf of Banc Joli, noting here a set of
wheels off some defunct bogie, there a stove-in boiler tank. And
though I shouldn't really have done it, but pressed on, I allowed
myself a saunter through the buildings which were lit up by low
sun – the foundry, the smithy, the pattern shop. In each section
there was a trace of former activity – in the smithy, more than a
trace. An outsize punctured bellows waited to revive fire on the
hearth which would never be warm again. Because of the time of
day, though, you couldn't feel melancholy there. The glow inside
was a surprise considering the windows were screened with
pierced metal sheeting. Hexagon lattice. Yellow light passed
through them like the sand used in the foundry for casting from
patterns. I've used that metaphor the wrong way round. Their
materials were cool sand, hot molten iron.

Instead of filling a beach-bucket, the workmen packed a
wooden mould. The resulting sand pies were replicas (in negative)
of any needed item – batches of damp sand 'boxes' into which the
seething metal ran. Later, when cold, the new spare part was lifted,
brushed clean, smoothed of irregularities; and the sand
presumably was used again, wetted and dried over and over like
the sands of the shore.

I stayed for a good while, working this out to my satisfaction before I left – made the most of the place. But, onward! Or I should be forced to quit.

The cutting in the mountain face narrowed and became the line of the old quarry railway, reduced to a crumbling track-bed. Soon there was real risk of falling. Yet when one stood and gazed it was almost possible to believe in unpowered flight; mentally one made the test of the air-streams. Sink or soar? If one must fall, it would surely be to part the waters as cleanly as a bird and continue diving, diving the mirror-image of flying . . . As a rule I suffer from vertigo. But I think this feat must be the mirror-image of a great arrogance, huge aspirations.

It was literally a strategic site, up here. This look-out stance had something timeless about it, with visual command of the Straits and the Irish Sea, of the coast for many miles both east and west.

Only from such heights could early man survey the scene – any pre-aeroplane man, in fact. For him the fascination of high places wasn't simply military or speculative: it involved metaphysics. Utmost temptation offered to Jesus Christ was shown from the top of a mountain. No helicopters then available. Ariel and Puck were powered by imagination and their author's memory of a view from a hill was magnified a thousandfold.

Late in the Day (1983)

Gwyn Jones
(1907-1999)

Gwyn Jones is one of the most significant figures in the literature of Wales in the twentieth century. He was a poet, novelist and scholar and the co-translator of the most widely read version of The Mabinogion.

I have come down from the hill fronting my home, in the griping end of January. Frost every night, some snow (but the salt air quickly shifts in), the beaked east wind splitting the crust of earth, so that a paradoxical dust is sifted into every hoof-mark. The brook runs still in its protected hollow, but in the Clarach valley puddles of rain which fell six weeks ago are ice, and from the hill-end look like a pattern of lime-heaps against the dull furrows. The sea is suddy and brown under a brown sky, the illimitabilities of the Bay are shrunk to a pond's breadth; to the east one can see saltings of snow in the folds of Plynlymon. Along the sky-line ahead a farmer in broken-nosed cloth cap and flapping army greatcoat leads a horse and cart to where he is dunging next year's pasture. Three dogs keep with him in single file on some narrow ribbon of track which is probably a rabbit run. I shout, and he shouts. Then a sheep bleats miserably. I round a gorse bush, and a ewe stands there in thin and grievous shelter. She has just dropped her lamb, and sways a little against the bush. The birth cord hangs from her like a tarred rope to the blood-wet youngster on the ground. What a day to choose! What a time, what a place! I shout again, and the farmer comes heavily across, his boots battering the wintry grass. The three dogs, one a worn old bitch with hanging wallow, sit solemnly around and sniff the air. This is *vieux jeu* to them. The bitch even yawns. The farmer stands and talks for a while when his job is done. Some sheep are wanderers, he assures me – as he has assured me before. High places and low, rock ledges over the sea – he wags his head at the goings-on of sheep. Before he goes back to his cart the lamb is trembling on its four legs, its head is tucked under the woollen valance, and its tail makes those furious frisks and firks which suggest that all goes well in not too bad a world.

'All this too, I thought, is Wales, and this is half of Wales.

A Prospect of Wales (1948)

Huw Jones

Journey

He is alone,
cradled by the rocking rhythm
of track, wrapped in a warm
shroud of cigarette smoke,
skating unnoticed
into the waiting dusk.

Scraps of sleet
bandage the broken scalp.
In the dark heart of the wood
winter creeps with polecat
claws to clot the veins
and snap the bones
like dead twigs.

Sleet has turned to rain
and racks his face in the window.
A few farms
wink in the distant
mountain and the mole
scurries through the darkness.

Francis Kilvert
(1840-1879)

Kilvert's Diary *is an enduringly popular work evoking, as it does, life in a rural border parish in the second half of the nineteenth century.*

As curate of Clyro in the old county of Radnor, Francis Kilvert walked to every corner of the parish in the course of his pastoral work. It was a static, stable world until the forces of change swept away that way of life quite early in the last century.

In the following extract he makes an ascent of Cader Idris and it is interesting to compare his account with that written over a century earlier by Richard Warner. See page 120.

As we sloped up the mountain side we had beautiful views of the Harlech mountains opposite, blue Cardigan Bay and dim Snowdon. The zig-zag path was steep in parts and a great wind blew over the mountain so that I had to sit down in a sheltered place and tie the band of my hat to my button-hole with the old guide's neckerchief, for, said the old man, 'Many hats have been lost on this ridge'. We aimed for a great stone on the top of the first ridge. After this the climbing was not so severe. The old man came up very slowly. Soon after we passed the great stone we passed through a gateway the posts of which were large basaltic pillars. Here we saw a mountain standing apparently·close by waiting upon Cader Idris. It was Plynlimmon. Here we passed round over the back of the mountain and began ascending the summit from the S. We came to a little round pool, or rather hole, full of water. The old man pulled a little tumbler out of his pocket, rinsed it, and gave me a glass of the clear bright water. It was delicious. Then he drank himself. He said the pool was the head water or spring of the Dysyni River. He had never known it dry in the driest summers. We saw from the spring the winding gleam of the Dysyni wandering down a desolate valley to join the Dyfi, its sister stream.

About this time the wind changed and flew suddenly round into the S. The head of Idris, which had been cowled in cloud, had cleared for a while, but now an impenetrable dark cloud settled down upon it and the mist came creeping down the mountain. The sky looked black and threatened rain. Now there lay before us vast tracts and belts of large stones lying so close together that no turf could be seen and no grass could grow between them. It was broken basalt, and huge lengths of basalt, angled, and some hexagonal, lay about or jutted from the mountain side like enormous balks of timber and with an unknown length buried in the mountain. We passed quarries where some of the great columns had been dug out to be drawn down the mountain on sledges. Cader Idris is the stoniest, dreariest, most desolate mountain I was ever on. We came now to the edge of a vast gulf or chasm or bason almost entirely surrounded by black precipices rising from the waters of a small black tarn which lay in the bottom of the bason. Here the guide showed me the place at the foot of an opposite precipice where Mr Smith's body had been found. Then we stumbled and struggled on again over rough tracts and wildernesses of slate and basalt. The sun was shining on the hills below, but the mist crawled down and wrapped us as if in a shroud, blotting out everything. The mists and clouds began to sweep by us in white thin ghostly sheets as if some great dread Presences and Powers were going past, and we could only see the skirts of their white garments. The air grew damp and chill, the cloud broke on the mountain top and it began to rain. Now and then we could discern the black sharp peak which forms the summit looming large and dark through the cloud and rain and white wild driving mist, and it was hidden again. It is an awful place in a storm. I thought of Moses on Sinai.

The rain grew heavier. The old guide could not get on very fast and told me to go on alone to the top and shelter in the hut as I could not miss the path. So I went on up the last sharp peak looming through the dark mist and cloud, by a winding path among the great rocks and wildernesses of loose stone. For a few minutes I was alone on the top of the mountain. The thought struck me, suppose the old man should be seized with cramp in the stomach here, how in the world should I get him down or get down myself in the blinding mist? The cloud and mist and rain swept by and drove eddying round the peak. I could hear the old man clinking his iron-shod staff among the rocks and stones, as he came up the path, nearer and nearer, but till he got close to me I could not discern his white figure through the dense mist. 'This is the highest point of Cader Idris,' he said, laying his hand upon a peak of wet living rock, 'not that,' looking with contempt at the great conical piles of stones built upon the peak by the sappers and miners during the Ordnance Survey. He said, 'The Captain of the surveying company had his tent pitched on the top of Cader Idris for three summer months and never left the place. He had 18 men to wait upon him. And how many clear views do you think he got in that tie?' 'Twelve,' I hazarded. 'Nine,' he said.

He took me down to a rude 2-roomed hut built of huge stones by his father just under the shelter of the peak, and produced for my benefit a hard-boiled egg and some slices of bread and butter. Also he gave me a woollen comforter to wrap round my neck. Then he vanished. The mist drove in white sheets and shapes past the doorless doorway and past the windows from which the window frames had been removed and the wind whistled through the chinks in the rude walls of huge stones. A large flat block of stone in the middle of the room on which I sat formed the table. It is said that if one spends a night alone on the top of Cader Idris he will be found in the morning either dead or a madman or a poet gifted with the highest degree of inspiration. Hence Mrs Hemans' fine song 'A night upon Cader Idris'. The same thing is said of the top of Snowdon and of a great stone at the foot of Snowdon. Old Pugh says the fairies used to dance near the top of the mountain and he knows people who have seen them.

Presently, I heard the old man clinking his stick among the rocks and coming round the hut. He came in and lighted his pipe and we prepared to go down by the 'Foxes Path'. And indeed it was a path fit only for foxes. After leading me a few steps he began to go over what seemed to me to be the edge of a precipice, depth unknown and hidden in the mist. The side of the mountain was frightfully steep here and required great care in going down. Suddenly the old man stopped at a beautiful little spring in the almost perpendicular bank, pulled out his tumbler and gave me a draught of clear sparkling water, much colder than the water from the spring of Dysyni. About the spring the grass grew brilliant green and there was a long winding riband of bright green where the waters overflowing from the spring trickled down through the grass stems to feed the lake at which the foxes drink just below. Next we came to a broad belt of loose rocks lying close together which the guide cautioned me to beware of and not without reason saying they were as slippery as glass and that a sprained ankle was an awkward thing on the mountain. Down, down and out of the cloud into sunshine, all the hills below and the valleys were bathed in glorious-sunshine – a wonderful and dazzling sight. Above and hanging overhead the vast black precipices towered and loomed through the clouds, and fast as we went down the mist followed faster and presently all the lovely sunny landscape was shrouded in a white winding sheet of rain. The path was all loose shale and stone and so steep that planting our alpenstocks from behind and leaning back upon them Alpine fashion we glissaded with a general landslip, rush and rattle of shale and shingle down to the shore of the Foxes' Lake. The parsley fern grew in sheets of brilliant green among the grey shale and in the descent we passed the largest basaltic columns of all protruding from the mountain side. In the clefts and angles of the huge grey tower columns grew beautiful tufts and bunches of parsley fern. We passed another lake, and after some rough scrambling walking over broken ground at the mountain foot, we came back into the turnpike road at the lake that we had passed in the morning. As we entered Dolgelley the old man said, 'You're a splendid walker, Sir,' a compliment which procured him a glass of brandy and water.

Diary (1938-40)

Charles Kingsley
(1819-1875)

Kingsley's fiction is characterised by the expression of the middle class morality of his period and by the sense of melodrama which we tend to associate with nineteenth century writing.

Here the landscape of Snowdonia can be seen as an extension of the state of mind of the character Elsley, an anguished individual.

Elsley left the door of Pen-y-gwryd, careless whither he went, if he went only far enough.

In front of him rose the Glyder Vawr, its head shrouded in soft mist, through which the moonlight gleamed upon the chequered quarries of that enormous desolation, the dead bones of the eldest-born of time. A wild longing seized him; he would escape up thither; up into those clouds, up anywhere to be alone – alone with his miserable self. That was dreadful enough; but less dreadful than having a companion – ay, even a stone by him – which could remind him of the scene which he had left; even remind him that there was another human being on earth beside himself. Yes – to put that cliff between him and all the world! Away he plunged from the high road, splashing over boggy uplands, scrambling among scattered boulders, across a stormy torrent bed, and then across another and another:- when would he reach that dark marbled wall, which rose into the infinite blank, looking within a stonethrow of him, and yet no nearer after he had walked a mile?

He reached it at last, and rushed up the talus of boulders, springing from stone to stone; till his breath failed him, and he was forced to settle into a less frantic pace. But upward he could go, and upward he went, with a strength which he never had felt before. Strong? How should he not be strong, while every vein felt filled with molten lead; while some unseen power seemed not so much to attract him upwards, as to drive him by magical repulsion from all that he had left below?

So upward and upward ever, driven on by the terrible gad-fly, like Io of old he went; strumbling upwards along torrent beds of slippery slate, writhing himself upward through crannies where the waterfall splashed cold upon his chest and face, yet could not cool the inward fire; climbing, hand and knee up cliffs of sharp-edged rock; striding over downs where huge rocks lay crouched in the grass, like fossil monsters of some ancient world, and seemed to stare at him with still and angry brows. Upward still, to black terraces of lava, standing out hard and black against the grey cloud, gleaming, like iron in the moonlight, stair above stair, like those over which Vathek and the princess climbed up to the halls of Eblis. Over their crumbling steps, up through their cracks and crannies, out upon a dreary slope of broken stones, and then – before he dives upward into the cloud ten yards above his head – one breathless look back upon the world.

Two Years Ago (1857)

R.M. Lockley

Ronald Lockley is well known for his pioneering work in the field of natural history. He combines this interest with a considerable literary talent. He is the author of many books, including The Way To An Island. *In this extract he describes a walk which he took around parts of the South Wales countryside when he was a teenager.*

I found a road going down to the Usk at Crickhowell. And invited by the tree-shaded lane, I marched north, intending to settle for the night in the Black Mountains, which I knew were free of collieries, and but sparsely inhabited by shepherds. I bought two loaves and some butter at Crickhowell, and took the road which passes through Cwm on its way to Talgarth. I still had ten shillings on me, and so there was no need to work just yet. It would be good just to get as far as possible from home, and then, with my clothes more ragged and my need greater, I could look into the matter of earning my keep.

So, with buzzards overhead and a song-thrush singing in the bottom of the valley, I ate my lunch, and then moved up the long west valley of the Black Mountains. How hard, even with a woodlark singing on a low hill, was it to keep my thoughts off home. When the sun vanished behind the western mountains I was on the pass, looking north to Talgarth, and a freezing wind coming from that direction. Soon snow began to fall, thinly and then in large driving flakes.

The shepherds on the mountains had been busy all day driving sheep to the lower fields, and now I realized why.

I turned back to the last farm, and begged the use of the hay loft for the night. An aged Welsh woman answered that I might have it – at least that is how I interpreted her mumbling English. I gathered that the master was away, and that I was not welcome to share the bright wood fire which I could just see through the half-open inner door. She shut the outer door, and left me feeling strangely lonely and weary. I made my way to the well-filled hay loft, and climbed by a ladder to the top of a rick. There, against a windowless opening for the sake of the dying light, I burrowed a bed for myself deep in the warm sweet-smelling hay. A flutter of snowflakes came in now and then on a gust of wind. The farm dog, which had barked ceaselessly at first, gradually gave up and, with a few last growls, went back to the old woman.

The Way to an Island (1941)

Wilson MacArthur

The road ran straight uphill, beyond a gate; it swept upwards through a steep valley towards the green hill crests, a brave, stout-hearted road determined to conquer the height, an inviting road that was yet challenging. The other road swung off to the right below the gate, sweeping into a little valley that hid the bus' destination, Cwm Swch, the 'dry dingle' nestling among green hills.

We opened the gate and went through and faced the steep valley.

The sun was warm, the air sparkling clear, and far away appeared the remote shape of a cottage, high above us. That cottage should be our first objective. On our right the ground sloped steeply to the stream that clucked and plashed over grey stones as it tumbled down the valley – the Afon y Foel that was to lead us up to the great moors.

As we climbed our packs grew heavier. They contained the minimum requirements for a month or more and as this was Wales, and a mountainous part of Wales at that, there were the essentials to secure us against driving rain and bitter chill. We had need of none of them; yet we could not know that, else we should have travelled lightly indeed.

The road challenged; but there was no cause for haste. There is a disadvantage in walking down a river instead of up, for to reach the source is always the hardest part, yet when you are fresh at starting it takes time to fall into the swing of tramping, to grow accustomed to a weight on your back.

The River Conway (1952)

Arthur Machen
(1863-1947)

Machen, who was born in Caerleon-on-Usk, wrote fiction in which he sometimes drew on visions of the Celto-Romantic past or, by complete contrast, the evils of the London streets. His short story 'The Shining Pyramid' is for me one of the most vividly written tales of human evil.

The following extract is taken from Far Off Things, *a volume of autobiography.*

. . . from the heart of this London atmosphere I was suddenly transported in my vision to a darkling, solitary country lane as the dusk of a November evening closed upon it thirty long years before. And, as I think that the pure provincial can never understand the quiddity or essence of London, so I believe that for the born Londoner the country ever remains an incredible mystery. He knows that it is there – somewhere – but he has no true vision of it. In spite of himself he Londonises it, suburbanises it; he sticks a gas lamp or two in the lanes, dots some largish villas of red brick beside them, and extends the District or the Metropolitan to within easy distance of the dark wood. But here was I carried from luminous Oxford Street to the old deep lane in Gwent, which is on the borders of Wales. Nothing that a Londoner would call a town within eight miles, deep silence, deep stillness everywhere; hills and dark wintry woods growing dim in the twilight, the mountain to the west a vague, huge mass against a faint afterlight of the dead day, grey and heavy clouds massed over all the sky. I saw myself, a lad of twenty-one or thereabouts, strolling along this solitary lane on a daily errand, bound for a point about a mile from the rectory. Here a footpath over the fields crossed the road, and by the stile I would wait for the postman.

Far Off Things (1922)

Gwilym Marles
(1834-1879)

Gwilym Marles (William Thomas) was an uncle to Dylan Thomas' father and spent a considerable period of his life at Llandysul. He was a unitarian minister and a radical writer.

Visit to Llwynrhydowen

The grass grows on the pathways –
That once were spruce and clean,
And yet it grows quite slowly,
A pale and spindly green,
As if ashamed to cover
The footprints that were cast
By all the saints who came here
To worship in the past.

Gwilym Marles
Translated by John Edwards

John Mawdsley

The author was the leader of a party from Liverpool who visited Flintshire in 1845 on an excursion. The highlight of the visit was an ascent to the summit of Moel Fammau, which divides the highest of the Clwydian hills between Flintshire and Denbighshire.

. . . we parted with our little guide, to whom we gave sixpence, a present with which the poor girl appeared very much pleased, and ascended the last steep of the hill, when the two boys commenced in good earnest picking the bilberry, a black-looking fruit, similar in appearance when in numbers at a little distance to the black currant, and which grows on a small stunted looking shrub of upright stem and smooth leaves, the botanical name of which is *Vaccinium myrtillus*, which flowers in May; its fruit ripening in the latter end of July and beginning of August. On our return, we partook of a draught of the water of a spring, high up the mountain, which, clear as crystal, was very cold and rather hard. Thus we partook of the natural food yielded by the mountain, in meat and drink.

We at last mounted the crest of Moel Fammau, and passed through the obelisk, which has an opening to each cardinal point, a structure by no means creditable to the builders, whatever may be the opinion as to the design, considering its exposed situation, and which was to have stood as a memento of the jubilee of our revered monarch,, King George III, – 'twas said, – for ever. This building will, in a few years, unless means be taken to repair, or rather rebuild it, be a heap of rubbish, the south-eastern corner having given way throughout its height from its base, and fallen down, and the north-western corner is giving way and bulging out.

The top of this mountain is said to be 1,845 feet above the level of the sea, and the obelisk upon it 150 feet. We were told that the currents of air passing over the mountain were so irregular, and so varying in altitude, that the men working at the lower part of the structure, or ascending it, were at times subjected to such violent gusts of wind as almost to break the ladders they worked upon, when, higher up, it was partially calm; the reverse would as frequently be the case. From this mountain there is said to be a beautiful view of the Vale of Clwyd; but the morning of our visit was cloudy, and when the mid-day sun occasionally broke through, the effect below was as the drying of a damp sheet, the vapour would arise and obscure and view the more.

The Legend of St Winifed
or *A Trip to Flint, Halkyn and Holywell* (1845)

John Moore
(1907-1967)

Moore, who was a native of Tewkesbury, was the author of a number of titles on the countryside and rural life. These include the three novels which make up what has become known as the Brensham trilogy.

As a young man he wrote two supremely readable travel books, now unfortunately long out of print, The Welsh Marches *and* Tramping Through Wales.

Half of the art of walking is the art of travelling light. You can tell a novice by looking inside his kit-bag. The practised walker excludes from his kit everything which is not *absolutely necessary*; and he achieves a greater degree of comfort with little kit than the novice does with all his luxuries.

The walker chooses his company as carefully as he chooses his kit – and as selectively. Sometimes he feels that his own rucksack is the best company in the world. At others he travels with his best friend, but he knows that he is taking a risk in doing so, for walking – and particularly camping – is the sternest and most exacting test of friendship, and by walking in company most men have lost more friends than they have made. If a man can camp successfully with a woman, then he had better marry the girl and have done with it; for he has found the perfect wife.

But although you should *walk* alone or with one good friend, you may agreeably *hike* in the company of four or five or even a dozen; for hiking, being an affair of sweat and shoeleather, makes no intellectual demands upon companionship. After all, if you are going to spend your days in tearing breathlessly along a hard road, with blisters on your feet and an ache in your shoulders and forty pounds of kit on your back, you will not care very much what sort of fellows are tearing along beside you; and so you need choose them no more carefully than you would choose your company for a game of rounders.

With regard to your route – if you are a hiker, it matters not. You may indulge in your peculiar form of athletics anywhere. You may sweat, you may skin the soles of your feet, you may tire yourself out, in almost any part of the world. But if you are a walker, you will get away from the main roads and take to the woods, the mountains and the moors.

The Welsh Marches (1933)

I pitched my tent that evening at the edge of a coppice through which a tiny stream dripped musically. Then I sought out the village inn at Halkin, where I talked with two merry-faced farm-labourers and told them where I was going and the places which I should visit as I walked through Wales. I must be a great one for travelling, they said, and a fine walker, if I was going as far as all that . . . They complimented me on my Welsh accent. 'Hear how he says "Beddgelert" and "Rhyd-y-mwyn"!' Then I added to my growing reputation by swearing forcibly in Welsh when I upset my beer. 'Well, well,' they said, 'he knows a great deal, does he not? Wonder if he know this?' The older and merrier of the two then recited some lengthy obscenity and winked at his companion.

'Do you know that, eh?' he said to me.

'No. What does it mean?'

'Ha, ha! I do not think I will tell you. You might go saying it to the girls. Maybe you're lonely, all by yourself in the night-time!'

Then the two old satyrs prodded each other in the ribs and roared with laughter; and we all had another drink before I went back to my tent to cook my supper.

At Denbigh I ate bread-and-cheese at an inn; and there I met a man from Liverpool who had climbed with Mallory and for whom, as for me, Mallory was still one of the Heroes. And so we talked of rocks and mountains and Alpine ice until three o'clock struck and the landlord turned us out.

The result of all this talk about climbing was that I drank much more beer than I should otherwise have done; and as a consequence of that I seemed to stride half-way to St Asaph with seven-league boots, and to drag myself for the other part with feet as heavy as lead. When the fine ecstasy left me I felt muzzy sick; and I had an incipient blister on my heel which hurt me at every step.

Tramping through Wales (1931)

Jan Morris

Jan Morris is most frequently referred to as a 'travel writer', a term which she herself would be the first to dismiss. Although her writing embraces travel she has also written extensively in the genres of history, biography and fiction.

People travelled immense distances to hear the great revivalists. Hundreds came by sea from north Wales to Daniel Rowlands at Llangeitho, landing at one or other of the little havens of the west coast and walking the rest of the way, and one of Wales' favourite stories tells of the sixteen year old Mary Jones, who walked fifty miles barefoot over the hill-tracks from her home in the Gwynedd mountains to get a copy of the Bible from the celebrated Thomas

Charles.

Wales: Epic Views of a Small Country (1998)

Leslie Norris

A February Morning

This February morning, walking early to work
Across the frost-hung fields where the mild cattle
Stand wreathed in their own breath, I watch smooth
Starlings, loud handfuls of shot silk,
And hear my steps echo on the iron rime of the time.
Just as they echoed so sharply time out of mind ago
In my own country's cold
On the Dowlais moors at the dark of night
With one fierce unnatural star
Alone in the sky's arch.
Along the uncertain edge of the hanging mountain
The wild ponies limped and trembled,
Ice chiming like bells
In the long hair of their flanks. My footsteps,
Picked clean out of the cold and country air,
Hung their thin images on the ear's sharpness
For miles along the road
With never a near light nor comfortable sound.

But gently, and from no apparent direction,
The voice of a singing woman used the air,
Unhurried, passionate, clear, a voice of grief
Made quite impersonal by the night and hour.
For full five minutes' space along that mountain,
Not loudly nor ever fading away,
A full voice sang
Of such inhuman longing that I no more
Can say which was the song or which the fiery star.
One or the other lit the hollow road
That lay behind my clipped and winter steps
Time out of mind ago, in Wales.

This frosty morning, across the February fields
The militant bush of the sun in tawny splendour
Has not extinguished it, that song or star.

William T. Palmer

Most impressive of all was the thunder of surf, the eerie whistling
and plucking of wind, when on a Christmas night, I walked the
path out to the Stacks at Holyhead. The day had been
disappointing; the haze had never lifted from the shore, no
unusual birds had appeared, the air was gloomy and discouraging.
At sunset a thin draught from the north-east 'blew the stars clear',
and over the tumbling sea was a thin crescent of moon. The sea-
cliff to the south was somewhat sheltered, and there I paused,
watching the play of moonbeams and starlight on the moving
breast of ocean, and listening to the regular crash of breaker and
the small fire of waves pushing through the gap between the South
Stack and the main cliff. A great liner went past with every port-
hole gleaming; it was hurrying into the Mersey so that passengers
and crew might snatch at least a remnant of the Christmas revels.
Nearer at hand passed the navigating lights of a coaster or such-
like vessel, outward bound, and almost in gloom.

As I scrambled back to the open road, the moon set, and the
mightily star pageant of the heavens became really splendid. High
above, I heard the call of passing birds, and remembered the
words of the cottager who was also a nature lover:

'When the air clears, there will be frost in the north, and the
bird flocks will fly over, going west to Ireland.'

This Isle of Anglesey is on a flight-line of migrants, both in
summer and in winter. The birds also pass over the Isle of Man
and up the western sea lochs of Scotland.

The man was, however, more concerned with the death-roll of
sea-birds in the last storm when the sands beneath the cliffs were
dotted with the bodies of kittiwakes, puffins, razorbills, guillemots
and other birds of cliff and shore. Most of these birds spend their
winters far out at sea, and return to their nesting-haunts in spring
and early summer, but a severe storm will drench their plumage
and beat them down into the waves. The corpses cast ashore are

numbered by scores at times, and in their decay they attract carrion and other crows, ravens, as well as the big gulls, from the whole island.

This cottager has only once crossed Menai Strait, and then merely to visit Caernarvon which he described to me as a wonderful emporium of the world's goods. He was well-read in English and Welsh, but he was a man of peace, and unspeakably pained when he found two authorities in conflict, even in print. 'Why can't they be in agreement?' he complained. 'The truth never changes.'

Down off the Lleyn peninsula, the Christmas sojourner may have a telescope glimpse of some small member of the whale family, but they do not come near the shore. The storms either drive the fish away or to unreachable depths, and the big animals come within sight of land. The porpoise, however, is fairly common, and a part of them can make as much fuss on the water as a larger whale.

Naturally I do not recommend the storm-battered cliffs and bays of Wildest Wales as a winter resort for the casual visitor. Wind, rain and fog often make progress difficult and dangerous, and the paths are exposed, rough and broken. A whirl off the rising tide reaches far up the cliffs, and may splash in a copious wave over the topmost edge. However, there are men and women, nature-lovers, who are prepared to go out and wrestle with hard weather for sheer love of the game, to fight through wind and to peer through sweeping rain and mist, happy in the present hour, and happier if some unusual bird or creature, some glorious effect of tide, cliff or moonlight comes their way.

In the following passage the author visits Llŷn on a December day.

The most glorious seaside memories are attached to the old paths along the cliffs. They are rugged, steep, and often enough slippery, and scramble from the sands and shingle right up to the realm of wild thyme and eyebright, of bracken and sweet heather, of ragwort and scabious and milkwort. Down in the cloven bay the tide sucks and washes among the rocks and caverns, and the ozone is enriched by aroma of decaying seaweed and bladder-wrack, but up on the cliff is freshness, strength, spaciousness, freedom, and a sense of comradeship with the elements of air, sea and land.

On a stormy day, walking along the cliffs is a strenuous task. I have seen the jagged rocks of Braich y Pwll coated with ice, with spray sweeping high and freezing as it fell among the short grass. The tideway to the Isle of Bardsey was impassable, and might be for weeks, and I wondered how that isolated community would spend their Christmas. I had come down the Pilgrim Way, on which the last resting-places were the villages of Beddgelert and Clynnog Fawr, and as the roaring strait was faced, I understood why the ancient folks held that, even from Wales, two pilgrimages to Bardsey equalled one to Rome. The landing-place of the monks was buried by tumbling seas, and cataracts of foam, flying high above, drifted over the smoother patch which is all that remains of the chapel of the Virgin where pilgrims prayed for courage and safety in making the dangerous crossing.

'More Odd Corners of North Wales'

For seventeen miles the Pilgrim's Road to Bardsey goes through quiet parishes like Tydweiliog and Penllech, to Four Crosses, then along the Meyllteyrn-Aberdaron road to 'the last village in North Wales'. The final lane to Braich-y-Pwll is narrow and often floored with bare rock. There are more views of bays and cliffs in its two miles than there was in the seventeen miles from Nevin to Aberdaron. At the end the common is entered, and in ten minutes one walk (cars are not permitted) down the long green track to the levelled space where tradition says was built the chapel of St Mary, for the fortification in religious courage, if such were needful of the pilgrims who now had to descend into a deep rock cove and get on board the hide-covered boats or curraghs of the monks of Bardsey. The isle is about two miles away, and the sea seems always stirring in the strait. The landing-place is impossible for a modern boat, yet it obviously was the correct way to the Isle of Saints. In a crevice of the rocks, cut off at high tide and during storm, is the triangular recess into which drips the fresh water of St Mary's Well. Traditions says that the devotee who takes a mouthful of water from this recess, and scrambles up the battered sea-cliffs to the altar of the church without swallowing or spilling a drop, was rewarded by the granting of his or her silent prayer. The rock scenery of Braich-y-Pwll is splendid: there are cliffs to Porth Oer to the north and to Aberdaron round the south which come in splendid succession. And the moors about Mynydd Mawr and

Mynydd Anelog are lonesome and free, with views to Anglesey, Ireland, and along Cardigan Bay to the distant headlands of Strumble and St David's, in Pembrokeshire. There are many seabirds among the rocks, and wonderful flowers among the grass.

At all times there is vision of Bardsey across the narrow strait. Many were the funeral processions which came in the days of Ancient Faith down the Pilgrim's Road, for it was held that to mingle the dust of a loved and honoured one with that of departed saints endowed it with peace. Meilir, a bard of the twelfth century, surely had this in mind when he sang, in his *Bards' Deathbed*:

Fair island of Mary! White isle of the Saints!
How blest to lie there against the day of uprising!

Wales (1932)

T.H. Parry-Williams
(1887-1975)

Oddly, and yet quite naturally, my starting point from home has always been downhill, and it was downhill that I went sadly enough to start at a new school for the first time, and to spend some weeks away from my family. The delights of expectancy had been long exhausted, and I hated feeling the hill drawing me, as it were, against my will, down to the valley, just as, later on, I hated its holding me back as I climbed up. But I had to get on with it now, and change districts for a time; I had started on my journey and had been escorted part of the way. Superficial smiles of bravery had accompanied the farewells, and I had walked the level mile or more to Pont Cae'r Gors before the real descent began. Near this bridge a new stream starts flowing to the sea, although the sea itself is not in sight. That September day the wind was blowing from the sea to the mountain, and on the top of the hill it came strongly and unashamedly into my face. My eyes became moist. In a flash I realised enviously in what direction it was blowing.

Ysgrifau, translated by Gwynn ap Gwilym

Thomas Love Peacock
(1785-1866)

Peacock married a daughter of the vicar of Maentwrog and came to know Wales. His style is sometimes ornate and always very distinctive. It has been said that he hoped to create an image of Wales akin to the way in which Scott creates an evokation of Scotland.

. . . They now emerged, by a winding ascent, from the vale of Llanberis, and after some little time arrived at Bedd Gelert. Proceeding through the sublimely romantic pass of Aberglaslynn, their road led along the edge of Traeth Mawr, a vast arm of the sea, which they then beheld in all the magnificence of the flowing tide. Another five miles brought them to the embankment, which has since been completed, and which, by connecting the two counties of Meirionnydd and Caernarvon excludes the sea from an extensive tract. The embankment, which was carried on at the same time from both the opposite coasts, was then very nearly meeting in the centre. They walked to the extremity of that part of it which was thrown out from the Caernarvonshire shore. The tide was now ebbing: it had filled the vast basin within, forming a lake about five miles in length and more than one in breadth. As they looked upwards with their backs to the open sea, they beheld a scene which no other in this country can parallel, and which the admirers of the magnificence of nature will ever remember with regret, whatever consolation may be derived from the probable utility of the works which have excluded the waters from their ancient receptacle. Vast rocks and precipices, intersected with little torrents, formed the barrier on the left: on the right, the triple summit of Moelwyn reared its majestic boundary: in the depth was that sea of mountains, the wild and stormy outline of the Snowdonian chain, with the giant Wyddfa towering in the midst. The mountain-frame remains unchanged, unchangeable; but the liquid mirror it enclosed is gone.

The tide ebbed with rapidity: the waters within, retained by the embankment, poured through its two points an impetuous cataract, curling and boiling in innumerable eddies, and making a tumultuous melody admirably in unison with the surrounding scene. The three philosophers looked on in silence; and at length unwillingly turned away, and proceeded to the little town of Tremadoc, which is built on land recovered in a similar manner from the sea. After inspecting the manufactories, and refreshing themselves at the inn on a cold saddle of mutton and a bottle of sherry, they retraced their steps towards Headlong Hall, commenting as they went on the various objects they had seen.

Headlong Hall (1816)

Pedestress and Sir Clavilene Woodenpeg

In a book with the formidable title A Pedestrian Tour of thirteen hundred and forty seven miles through Wales and England *the author, whoever he may have been, presents us with a tour account with a difference. His primary aim has been to entertain the reader and much of the pleasure and interest derives from the comic dialogue employed. Here we find two travellers in Montgomeryshire where they encounter an individual whom they quickly become averse to when he engages them in conversation.*

'If you please, sir,' he said with respect, either real of feigned, and making an awkward bow – 'If you please, sir – I beg pardon, sir, for the liberty I have taken in addressing you – Good morning, sir, it's a fine day – It's very warm, sir, this morning . . . '

'Yes,' answered Pedestres, cutting him short in his hesitating exordium; 'it's a fine day, and very warm'; and then was about to walk on. But the fellow had now broken the ice, and was determined to follow up the first step by a second.

'The roads have soon become dry and dusty, sir, since the rain,' he continued, with more freedom, yet great humility; and bringing himself up so as to walk by the side of his new acquaintance: 'and I think we shall have a turn of fine weather now, sir.'

'I think we shall.'

'And, sir, we have reason to hope so, for the hay-harvest is coming on:- we want dry weather.'

'We do.'

'They have already begun to mow the grass in many parts of the country.'

'I suppose they have.'

'This is a fine river, sir, here on our left.'

'Yes.'

'Do you know the name of it, sir?'

'Yes.'

Then succeeded a pause – 'How sweetly the little birds sing, sir,' he continued, finding that the other party was not disposed to renew the attack.

'Yes,' was the answer.

'Do you know what bird that is, sir, on the tree yonder?'

'No.'

'No more do I, sir.'

A pause –

'The farmers are very discontented with the crops, sir.'

'Are they!'

'There was too much rain in the beginning of the month.'

'I suppose so.'

'And it's too dry now, sir.'

'Indeed.'

'And it was too hot in May, sir.'

'Ah.'

Another pause. –

'I should think you were fond of walking, sir?'

(Now, thought Pedestres, he is touching more on the point.)

'Yes – I like walking.'

'And yet the Welsh proverb says – '*In* BEDESTR *anwybodaeth.*' – In a run-about there is ignorance, or a rolling stone collects no moss; and *Goreu* PEDESTR *yw gau,*' – the best foot-traveller is a false report.'

'I grieve I am no great proficient in Welsh.'

'But walking, sir, is good for the health.'

'Very.'

'Perhaps you have walked far, sir?'

'Perhaps I have.

'I should think you had walked a good way, sir?'

'Four hundred miles.'

'Sir!'

The man jumped a yard off the ground, as if he had been electrified.

'What, sir? – I beg your pardon, sir.'

'Four hundred miles.'

'Lor', sir – this *morning*, sir?'

'No.'

'I suppose you are travelling for pleasure, sir?'

'Or else for pain.'

'I shouldn't think for pain, sir – pain hurts you know.'

'Of course I don't travel without a reason.'

'Why, no, sir. – Or you might be travelling for some trade!'

'True – not impossible.'

'A great many trades employ travellers to go all over the country, sir.'

'I believe they do.'

'I thought you might be one of these, sir.'

'I thank you.'

'I beg your pardon, sir – and yet I thought you looked like a *jinnleman* too.'

Pedestres made him a low bow.

'And you carry your pack with you – '

'*Pack*, sir!'

'I beg your pardon, sir – '

'*Knapsack*, if you please.'

'I suppose, sir, you have got things in it, sir?'

'*Things*, sir? – yes, sir: I have got *things* in it, sir. It is not full of emptiness.'

'It's a very neat sack, sir.'

'*Sack! – knapsack*, if you please.'

'Oh yes, sir – I beg pardon. – It must be very convenient for carrying clothes and money in,' said the man, putting his hand upon it.

'Hands off, villain!' exclaimed Pedestres, starting round, and involuntarily feeling for the pistol that he carried in his bosom: 'Dare you touch me, or anything that belongs to me.'

The mad blood was up – Clavileno all agog – and in another instant the squire would have displayed a glittering foot of cold steel to the rays of the sun.

A Pedestrian Tour Through Wales and England (1836)

Thomas Pennant
(1726-1798)

As a naturalist and antiquary Pennant had no rivals and the extent of his achievement has, even now, not been as widely acknowledged as it deserves. His 'Tours in Wales' had a considerable influence on the literary tourists who visited and wrote about Wales in the late eighteenth and early nineteenth centuries and this is reflected by the number of times his name occurs in their works.

The way lies beneath that vast precipice, *Castell y Geifr*, or *The Castle of the Goats*. In some distant age, the ruins of a rocky mountain formed a road by a mighty lapse. A stream of stones, each of monstrous size, points towards the *Cwm*; and are to be clambered over by those only, who possess a degree of bodily activity, as well as strength of head to beat the sight of the dreadful hollows frequent beneath them.

Observe, on the right, a stupendous *roche fendue*, or split rock, called *Twll-Du*, and *The Devil's Kitchen*. It is a horrible gap, in the centre of a great black precipice, extending in length about a hundred and fifty yards; in depth, about a hundred, and only six wide; perpendicularly open to the surface of the mountain. On surmounting all my difficulties, and taking a little breath, I ventured to look down this dreadful aperture, and found its horrors far from being lessened in my exalted situation; for to it were added the waters of Llyn y Cwm, impetuously rushing through its bottom.

Reach Glyder Fawr and pass by the edge of Clogwyn Du Ymhen y Glyder, as dreadful a precipice as any in Snowdonia, hanging over the dire waters of Llyn Idwal. Its neighbourhood is of great note among botanists for rare plants . . . The prospect from this mountain is very noble. Snowdon is seen to great advantage; the deep vale of Llanberis and its lakes, Nant Ffrancon, and a variety of other similar views . . . Numerous groups of stones are placed almost erect, sharp pointed and in sheafs; all are weather-beaten, time-eaten, and honey-combed, and of a venerable grey colour. The elements seem to have warred against this mountain; rains have washed, lightnings torn, the very earth deserted it; and the winds made it the residence of storms, and style a part of it Carnedd y Gwynt, or The Eminence of Tempests.

'Tours in Wales' (1781)

Jim Perrin

Jim Perrin, who was born in Manchester, has achieved a considerable reputation as a climber and as a writer. Wales has for many years been his adoptive country. Professor M. Wynn Thomas writes that 'he deserves to be recognised as the most singular and the most outstanding prose writer of present day Wales'.
Here he describes an ascent of Cadair Idris.

Perhaps this is my favourite mountain, though I'm not sure: Brandon, Shivling, Rhobell Fawr – how are we to choose? Strength of association might lead me to Cadair, though. And, if so, there would be the pleasure of starting from Dolgellau. It is the oddest little town, piled-up and intricate, its grey stone and plain, elegant style taken from the mountain. Down on it, from 2,800 feet above, peer the summit crags of Mynydd Moel – easternmost of the trinity of great peaks that make up Cadair Idris. To linger in the National Milk Bar (an institution in every North and Mid-Wales town), listen to the playful conversation and admire the lovely faces of the local young women before setting out on a luminous winter's day maybe for the summits, is one of the pleasures of life. The Reverend Francis Kilvert – surely the most amiable of all our great diarists – did much the same thing in 1871: 'I was very much struck and taken with the waitress at the Golden Lion. She said her name was Jane Williams and that her home was at Betws-y-coed. She was a beautiful girl with blue eyes, eyes singularly lovely, the sweetest saddest most weary and most patient eyes I ever saw. It seemed as if she had a great sorrow in her heart.'

Kilvert took the Pony Track up Cadair by the Rhiw Gwredydd, but there's a better way. Fron Serth – the name means 'steep hill' and it is precisely that – on the outskirts of town leads up into an exquisite region of oakwoods, sheep pasture and little ridges at the north-eastern end of the Cadair range. Tir Stent, it's called on the map – Welsh landscape at its most typical and jewelled, looking out to Rhobell Fawr, which rises with an attractive symmetry from this angle above the valley of the Wnion. An old, flagged pony track runs through it over to the top of the Tal-y-llyn pass, and is a good way to gain the eastern gable of the longest and finest mountain ridge south of the Scottish border. The ascent to its first summit, Gau Graig, is a merciless 1,100 feet in the space of half a mile. The view opens out to the north and east with every foot gained. There is a steep and gravelly 500 feet of ascent from Gau

Graig up to the ridge's next tier at Mynydd Moel. When last here, I was dawdling up it as a friendly sheepdog came bounding down with two walkers in attendance, heading for the valley with huge sacks, on which were strapped ice-axes and crampons, though not so much as a rag or shred of snow was to be seen, even in the most northerly of gullies. They gave me a breezy, stern hello and strode off purposefully after the dog, who seemed as impatient at their progress as they were dismissive of mine. Within a few minutes I was on top of Mynydd Moel, with the world and its people scattering off in all directions.

If you have never been up Cadair from this eastern end then you have a delight in store. From the state of the paths, by far the greater number who do climb Cadair seem never to venture even so far as Mynydd Moel, which is a great hill in its own right, massive in presence as you approach it from the east. Its top is particularly fine, with a shelter-cairn and a little cockscomb of rocks above plunging crags. You can see from it straight down on to Dolgellau, a bare two miles away, and that gives you the clue as to why, in Elizabethan times, this was considered the highest mountain in the British Isles. Penygadair – highest point of the Cadair range – may only be 2,928 feet (892m) above sea level, but sea level is just down there. Dolgellau is at it. Ben Nevis may be half as high again but it is twice as far from the sea. Those sandflats and long, low saltings of the Mawddach estuary give Cadair its uplift, its subjective impression of height. It *feels* a tremendous mountain.

A Sense of Place (1998), edited by Roly Smith

W.H. Potts

No anthology of walking literature would be complete without the rural tramp. All the year round he trudged, proclaiming his awful independence; he trudged in the summer, overcoated and trousered, until the sweat shifted his winter's grime into black muddy ripples, away from the cities into the empty miles of Wales where he tabulated scenery into terms of pigsties or barns to sleep and well-mannered farms where the occupiers would not be too afraid to help him with hot water for making his tea.

'They'm be tight round 'ere,' the old tramp confided, 'I've been askin' for hot water for hours,' and he took in with a bitter glance some of the finest scenery in Wales, and indeed the tightness was not surprising, for houses were few, and isolated at night.

'There ain't many barns nor ricks to sleep in round 'ere neither,' he complained.

He did not appear to realize that the animals had to eat and live on the mountains, and that he might have to do the same if he kept plodding towards hill-farm country.

'But I got in all right out of the wet last night,' he continued. 'Durned cold and wet I was, and I found a pigsty by itself. There was four big black pigs in it, an' all lying on nice clean straw, it 'ad only been put down a day or two. So I kicks one of the big black 'uns off the straw and picks up a bundle for meself, an' I settled down in the other corner.'

Roaming Down the Wye (1949)

Sheenagh Pugh

What if this road

What if this road, that has held no surprises
these many years, decided not to go
home after all; what if it could turn
left or right with no more ado
than a kite-tail? What if its tarry skin
were like a long, supple bolt of cloth
that is shaken and rolled out, and takes
a new shape from the contours beneath?
And if it chose to lay itself down
in a new way; around a blind corner,
across hills you must climb without knowing
what's on the other side; who would not hanker
to be going, at all risks? Who wants to know
a story's end, or where a road will go?

Dewi Roberts

That most chauvinistic of Englishmen, Daniel Defoe, described the Vale of Clwyd as 'pleasant, fruitful, populous and delicious', although he kept to the low ground and did not venture on to the hills.

Anyone who makes the ascent will be rewarded by the panorama of double-naved churches, farms at the end of green lanes and the unmistakable sight of Denbigh Castle, still standing guard over the ancient town. Further to my right, I can pick out Rhuddlan Castle and the estuary of the Afon Clwyd. Beyond is Liverpool Bay and the ugly coastal sprawl of Rhyl and Abergele, and, such is the visual trick which light plays on the sea, that an oil terminal, some fifteen miles from shore assumes the appearance of a galleon.

Descending the hillside down a sheep track through shale and heather, I cross Offa's Dyke and later come to a rough stone track. Back on a remote tarmaced road, I pass Plas-yn-Llan, an attractive half-timbered house where the young Wordsworth stayed on two occasions. It was the home of Robert Jones, a fellow undergraduate, and from here they made the excursion on foot to Snowdonia, which the poet celebrates in 'The Excursion'.

Further down, in the basin of the Vale, is an ugly Methodist chapel, circa 1838, long deserted. It stands now as a useless memorial. Many years ago it was the meeting place for a pious deacon and a young woman from the nearby village. One day they were discovered by the minister in the act of physical love, and both were instantly banished. The building mocks love now, and the graves are obscured by thick ivy.

I pass a farm. In the yard, a stockily built man in blue overalls is getting into the cab of his tractor.

'Lovely day,' I sing out.

'Oh aye. Alright if you don't have to work, I suppose.' His expression is weary.

'But it can't be all work, even on a farm,' and my voice, I hope, is that of sweet reason.

His response, however, is to rev up his engine noisily before moving off.

The road takes me over Afon Clwyd. Close to an old stone bridge I see a heron in the low-lying meadowland. I watch it as it takes flight and disappears over a copse of trees. From a greater distance, I hear the cry of the curlew, surely the most lonely sound in the countryside. Swallows zigzag over the fields to left and right.

At Llanrhaeadr I leave the road opposite the pub and enter an area of ancient mixed woodland. It is good to leave the heat of the day and to walk beneath the green canopy above. The ground at my feet is dappled with sunlight which penetrates through the branches.

A well-trodden path takes me to St Dyfnog's well, which has been a place of pilgrimage for centuries. Those inquisitive eighteenth century antiquaries, Pennant and Fenton, came there, as, a century later, did Gerard Manley Hopkins. But nowadays the site is visited by tourists and local people exercising their dogs.

The well basin is four sided, and it is often assumed that it was constructed during the Roman period. But it seems that it was quite possibly a result of something of a cult for wells of healing in the eighteenth century, when one can imagine country people, and others, being deeply superstitious. St Dyfnog, is seems, probably lived in the sixth century, and his was an extremely austere life, standing under a free-flowing waterfall which, at that time, is reputed to have coursed down a very steep bank. He may have worn a horsehair loincloth with a heavy iron girdle attached.

I sit on a log and listen to water from a small stream, as it pours into the basin, gaze around and reflect on all I have seen today.

Within five minutes, I am on a further path which will take me the short distance to my front door.

Robert Roberts
(1834-1885)

Robert Roberts (Y Sgolor Mawr) was a cleric and scholar who was born in Denbighshire. He became an ordinated priest but circumstances made it necessary for him to give up his life as a curate and he then emigrated to Australia. However, he came back to Wales in 1875 and worked in the capacity of private tutor. While in Australia he had written his autobiography, although it did not appear until many years after his death. It is a long and fascinating book.

Here we find the wandering scholar in Anglesey.

It was a delightful summer morning, and my spirits were high as I trudged through the green lanes bounded by fields of luxuriant grass and waving corn. The appearance of the country was much like what I had seen in the eastern part of the island, flat, or gently undulating; farmhouses, whitewashed, were thickly studded around, and along the lanes were a good many cottages, also whitewashed, but not very clean within so far as a glimpse of the interior through the open doors might enable one to judge. The greatest drawback in the landscape was the general absence of trees; the hedges were mere earthen banks, here and there planted with gorse or broom, so that in spite of the richness of the soil and the populousness of the country, there was a barrenness about its appearance which was not pleasing. I passed two or three chapels, square, new, whitewashed, and ugly; one or two churches, not whitewashed, dilapidated, gray, and mouldy, stuck in the corners of fields and in other inaccessible places, as if they were never meant to be filled and that they were not filled was pretty evident. One was in the middle of a swamp which could be approached only by a causeway. I was curious to know how the people got to it in winter time, and especially how the corpses were ever got to the churchyard, but there was no one about from whom I might obtain information – indeed there was no house on either side for half a mile or more.

Life and Opinions of a Wandering Scholar (1923)

Julius Rodenberg

This German writer wrote of a period which he spent in Wales in 1856 and his account originally appeared in German in 1858. It is only within the last thirty years that it has been available in an English translation.

My daily walk was to the lakes, of which Llyn Peris remained my favourite. Under a green bush on its rocky shore I dreamed away the hours of the midday sun. In the rocky ravine above the lake was a quarry called the Raven's Crag. The stones rolled and thundered down from the heights – because of the distance it was impossible to distinguish the workmen. And as the stones crashed down without the cause being visible, and what with the restless movement and activity and banging and everything in the dazzling midday sun, against the colourless grey background with the green heather above and the shadows of clouds – one could imagine it was a ghost town awakened with secret life! Lower down it was much quieter and magically darker; the lake was steely blue and moved only when the wind blew over it.'

An Autumn in Wales,
translated and edited by William Linnard (1985)

John Ruskin
(1819-1900)

Ruskin's role as an art critic was outstanding, and his seminal work Modern
Painters *is an invaluable contribution to the subject. His architectural writings
in* The Stones of Venice *was equally influencial.*

My first sight of bolder scenery was in Wales; and I have written –
more than it would be wise to print – about the drive from
Hereford to Rhaeadr, and under Plynlimon to Pontarfynach: the
joy of a walk with my father in the Sunday afternoon towards
Hafod, dashed only with some alarmed sense of the sin of being so
happy among the hills . . .

From Pontarfynach we went north, gathering pebbles on the
beach at Aberystwyth, and getting up Cader Idris with help of
ponies: it remained, and rightly, for many a year after, a king of
mountains to me. Followed Harlech and its sands, Ffestiniog, the
pass of Aberglaslyn, and marvel of Menai Straits and Bridge . . .

And so on to Llanberis and up Snowdon, of which ascent I
remember, as the most exciting event, the finding for the first time
in my life a real 'mineral' for myself, a piece of copper pyrites! But
the general impression of Welsh mountain form was so true and
clear that subsequent journeys little changed or deepened it.

'Praeterita' (1885)

There is only one finer walk than the one from Barmouth to
Dolgellau and that is the one from Dolgellau to Barmouth.

'Praeterita' (1885)

Norman Schwenk

Pembrokeshire Cliff Hike

All that day I followed you miles and miles,
dogged and faithful, like a veteran husky
follows the leader of his team, her bottom
bobbing along beautifully through the landscape.
What a bottom and, Lord, what a landscape –
the view surreal, a constant, changing dream,
magic lantern of you, earth, sea and sky
thrown in three dimensions and perfect colour.
Hard as I walked, I never once got closer.
Here was no mirage but a solid picture,
constantly receding as I advanced,
fading and growing fainter with the twilight.
And though it disappeared in the dark night,
I feel your spirit ahead, still tugging me.

William Makepeace Thackeray
(1811-1863)

Thackeray may not be read as widely as certain other nineteenth century English writers nowadays but, such are the fluctuations of literary fashion that a further adaptation of Vanity Fair *for television could focus much interest on his work again. In his* Cockney Travels *he recalls a visit to Gwent.*

Presently we turned up a lane in which at a given place we were told to descend, and see the Wind Rock. This is one of the steepest of the rocks on the road and commands views from its summit stretching miles across land and water. The wood of the rock itself is beautiful, and a curious descent is practised down the almost perpendicular step by means of ingenious zig-zag walks and rude steps along which a guide leads you. It is a delightful walk – delightful as you walk and delightful, I must confess, when you have done; in the first place there are all sorts of rocks and trees and caverns and wonderful creeping plants to see, and secondly, the walk is long, slippery, steep, and not altogether agreeable to Cockney feet – a slip over a smooth root, or the giving way of a stone, might put an end to all bodily excursions for the future, whether up hill or down. I do not know the height of the Wind Cliff – the guide book says it is 'most awful' – hard to descend, still harder to mount: but there is a good-natured woman at the bottom who mounts most cheerfully for a shilling, and will do so many times in the day.

Cockney Travels (1842)

Edward Thomas
(1878-1917)

Thomas was born in London but both his parents came from Wales. His Welsh parentage is not apparent in most of his poetry but there is a memorable reference to the country in Roads. *In a letter he wrote of 'Helen, the lady of the Mabinogion who married Maxen and gave her name to the great old mountain roads – Sarn Helen they are all marked on the maps . . . She is known to mythologists as one of the travelling goddesses of the dusk'.*

Thomas' wife was named Helen, which may give the poem even further significance.

Roads

I love roads:
The goddesses that dwell
Far along invisible
Are my favourite gods.

Roads go on
While we forget, and are
Forgotten like a star
That shoots and is gone.

On this earth 'tis sure
We men have not made
Anything that doth fade
So soon, so long endure:

The hill road wet with rain
In the sun would not gleam
Like a winding stream
If we trod it not again.

They are lonely
While we sleep, lonelier
For lack of the traveller
Who is now a dream only.

From dawn's twilight
And all the clouds like sheep
On the mountains of sleep
The wind into the night.

The next turn may reveal
Heaven: upon the crest
The close pine clump, at rest
And black, may Hell conceal.

Often footsore, never
Yet of the road I weary,
Though long and steep and dreary,
As it winds on for ever.

Helen of the roads,
The mountain ways of Wales
And the Mabinogion tales
Is one of the true gods.

Abiding in the trees,
The threes and fours so wise
The larger companies,
That by the roadside be.

And beneath the rafter
Else uninhabited
Excepting by the dead;
And it is her laughter

At morn and night I hear
When the thrush cock sings
Bright irrelevant things,
And when the chanticleer

Calls back to their own night
Troops that make loneliness
With their light footsteps' press,
As Helen's own are light.

Now all roads lead to France
And heavy is the tread
Of the living; but the dead
Returning lightly dance:

Whatever the road bring
To me or take from me,
They keep me company
With their pattering,

Crowding the solitude
Of the loops over the downs,
Hushing the roar of towns
And their brief multitude.

Thomas wrote a number of prose works during the first decade of the last century, including a fine biography of the rural writer Richard Jefferies. He published Beautiful Wales *in 1905. To some it may seem over romanticised, but there can be no doubting Thomas' sincerity.*

He describes the uninformed critics of Wales as 'unmelodious and even disgusting' and goes on to affirm that the great disadvantage for them is 'that it is not in England'.

I went on, and was over the edge of this country, 'built to music and so not built at all', when the sun began to rise behind me. Before, a range of hills stood up against the cold sky with bold lines such as a happy child will draw who has much paper and a stout crayon, and looked so that I remembered the proverb which says, that if a man goes up Cader Idris at night, by dawn he is dead, or mad, or a poet. They were immense; they filled half the sky; yet in the soft light that felt its way glimmeringly, and as if fearfully, among their vast valleys and along their high crags, they looked like ruins of something fare more mighty; the fields also, on this side of them, and all the alder-loving streams and mossy woods, were but as the embers of something which the night had made and had only half destroyed before its flight. And it was with surprise that, as I took my eyes off the prospect and looked down and in the hedge, I saw that I was in a place where lotus and agrimony and vetch were yellow, and the wild rose continued as ever to hesitate between red and white.

It was not long possible to turn my back upon the rising sun, and when I looked round, I saw that the country I had left had been taken into the service of the dawn and was beautiful two miles away. Factory and chimney and street were bent in a rude circle round the sun, and were as the audience of some story-teller, telling a new tale – silent, solemn, and motionless, round a fire; and over them the blue clouds were silent, solemn, and motionless, listening to the same tale, round the sun.

When I went on towards the hills, they by that time looked as if they had never known the night; and sweet it was to pass, now and then, a thatched, embowered cottage, with windows open to the scented air, and to envy the sleepers within, while I could see and recognise the things – the sky and earth and air, the skylarks singing among the fading stars, and the last cuckoo calling in the silent, vast and lonely summer land – which make dreamless sleep amidst them so divine, I had long not known why. For half the day there was nothing to remember but sudden long views that led, happily, nowhere, among the clouds or the hills, and farms with sweetly smiling women, and jutting out of every hedge-bank a little pistyll of fair water, curving and shining in the heat, over a slice of stone or through a pipe, into the road. These things the memory has to work to remember. For, in truth, the day was but as a melody heard and liked. A child who, in the Welsh story, went to the land of the fairies, could only say that he had been listening to sweet airs, when he returned after a long stay.

Beautiful Wales (1905)

Gwyn Thomas
(1913-1981)

The novelist Gwyn Thomas was much admired not only in Wales but also in America. It does not come as any surprise to find certain critics using the term genius in summing up his literary output.

Down from the moorland come the wild ponies, creatures that roam the streets of Ebbw Vale in a kind of democratic brotherhood with the citizens. And sheep-dogs foxed by living in a world half pastoral, half industrial, trapped by their neuroses into not knowing exactly what they are supposed to be rounding up.

It was here, over the moorland, that Aneurin Bevan often walked. The moorland and the pub at the end of the outward stroll restored him after the tight, oppressive rounds of political disturbance, and all the problems of fuel, movement and direction could, for a momenr or two, be forgotten. This was the other side of his life, and one which explains his moods, the contradictions that scurried across his life like clouds across a sky. For the men of the valleys live in two worlds. They know, on the one hand, the noise, the disfigurements, the failures of industrial man, and just up the hillside over the ridge, a pastoral calm that has never seriously been breached.

Men like Bevan know there is no going back to the simplicity, the reliable goodness of fern-covered plateaux, ploughed fields, the companionship of animals, whom not even a politician needs to distrust. For it is not likely that the horse will be given the vote for some time yet. All the same, when a man has a paradise of trees and fields half an hour's walking distance from his own street, he is going to find it harder to accept that street if it is sunk too far below the level of dignity and delight he expects for his neighbours and himself. Once you have heard the lark, known the swish of feet through hill-top grass and smelt the earth made ready for the seed, you are never again going to be fully happy about the cities and the towns that man carries like a crippling weight upon his back.

A Welsh Eye (1964)

R.S. Thomas

Ninetieth Birthday

You go up the long track
That will take a car, but is best walked
On slow foot, noting the lichen
That writes history on the page
Of the grey rock. Trees are about you
At first, but yield to the green bracken,
The nightjar's house: you can hear it spin
On warm evenings; it is still now
In the noonday heat, only the lesser
Voices sound, blue-fly and gnat
And the stream's whisper. As the road climbs,
You will pause for breath and the far sea's
Signal will flash, till you turn again
To the steep track, buttressed with cloud.

And there at the top that old woman,
Born almost a century back
In that stone farm, awaits your coming:
Waits for the news of the lost village
She thinks she knows, a place that exists
In her memory only.
You bring her greeting
And praise for having lasted so long
With time's knife shaving the bone.
Yet no bridge joins her own
World with yours, all you can do
Is lean kindly across the abyss
To hear words that were once wise.

Thomas Traherne
(1637-1674)

Although Traherne was born in Hereford, where his father was a shoemaker, he has, along with Herbert and Vaughan, become inextricably associated with southern Powys and Gwent.

He is remembered not only as a poet but also as the author of prose mediatations in which he reveals his very deep belief in a God who will grant him access to the spiritual riches of the universe.

Walking

To walk abroad is, not with eyes,
But thoughts, the fields to see and prize;
Else may the silent feet,
Like logs of wood,
Move up and down, and see no good,
Nor joy nor glory meet.

Ev'n carts and wheels their place do change,
But cannot see; though very strange
The glory that is by:
Dead puppets may
Move in the bright and glorious day,
Yet not behold the sky.

And are not men than they more blind,
Who having eyes yet never find
The bliss in which they move:
Like statues dead
They up and down are carried,
Yet neither see nor love . . .

Observe those rich and glorious things;
The rivers, meadows, woods,and springs,
The fructifying sun;
To note from far
The rising of each twinkling star
For us his race to run.

A little child these well perceives,
Who, tumbling in green grass and leaves,
May rich as kings be thought.
But there's a sight
Which perfect manhood may delight,
To which we shall be brought.

While in those pleasant paths we talk
'Tis that towards which at last we walk;
For we may by degrees
Wisely proceed
Pleasures of love and praise to heed,
From viewing herbs and trees.

Richard Warner
(1763-1857)

Warner, who was born in London, is one of the most interesting and entertaining of the literary pedestrians who visited Wales during the Romantic period.

We had originally contemplated a naval career but when his ambition was not realised he settled for a clerical life. He undertook two walking tours of Wales and the following item is taken from the second of these. He is the main subject of Ruth Bidgood's poem Tourists *(page 23).*

. . . we began to ascend the western summit of Cader Idris, a task not only of labour, but of some peril also, it being a different route from that which travellers usually pursue; six hundred feet of steep rock, covered, indeed, with short grass; but so slippery as to render the footing very insecure. As we approached the top, the ascent became more abrupt, whilst the scene below us, of craggy rocks, perpendicular precipices, and an unfathomable lake, did not operate to lessen the alarm that a person, unaccustomed to so dangerous a situation, naturally feels. Our companion the mountaineer skipped on, the mean while, with the agility of a goat, and whilst C   and I were dumb with terror, descanted on the beauties of Cader Idris, the excellence of its mutton, and the delicacy of its trout, as coolly as if he had been in the public house where we originally found him. At length, after excessive labour, and repeated efforts, we gained the top of this noble mountain, and were at once amply recompensed for all the fatigue and alarm of the ascent. The afternoon was gloriously fine, and the atmosphere perfectly clear, so that the vast unbounded prospect lay beneath us, unobscured by cloud, vapour, or any other interruption to the astonished and delighted eye; which threw its glance over a varied scene, including a circumference of at least five hundred miles. To the north-west is seen Ireland, like a distant mist upon the ocean; and a little to the right, Snowdon and the other mountains of Caernarvonshire. Further on, in the same direction, the Isle of Man, the neighbourhood of Chester, Wrexham, and Salop; the sharp head of the Wrekin, and the undulating summit of the Clee hills. To the south we have the country round Clifton, Pembrokeshire, St David's, and Swansea; and to the westward, a cast prospect of the British Channel unfolds itself, which is bounded only by the horizon. Exclusive of these distant objects, the nearer views are wonderfully striking. Numberless mountains, of different forms, appearances, and elevation, rise in all directions around us; which, with the various harbours, lakes and rivers, towns, villages, and seats, scattered over the extensive prospect, combine to form a scene inexpressibly august, diversified, and impressive. Having refreshed ourselves with the contents of a knapsack carried by our companion, we proceeded, in an eastern direction to the Pen-y-Cader, the highest peak of the mountain, passing on our left the *saddle* of the giant Idris, (from whom the mountain receives its name) and immense *cwm*, its bottom filled with a beautiful lake called Llyn Cair, and its sides formed by perpendicular cliffs at least 1000 feet in height. Here we found the Alpine grasses, the *Aira Caespitosa*, and the *Poa Alpina*; beautiful masses of spar, specimens of pyritae, and a stone much resembling that colcanic substance called pumice-stone. We were now upon the apex of the second mountain in Wales, in point of height, and 2850 feet above the green, near the neighbouring town of Dolgellau.

. . . Still we kept on, and still without success, till perplexed by intersecting roads, which every step grew less perceptible, we at length found ourselves at the top of a mountain, perfectly at a loss how to proceed. Rambling on for some time, we discovered a solitary cottage . . . to this we directed our steps and were fortunate enough to find the family at home, consisting of a man, his wife, and sister. The first spoke a little English; and (after understanding from whence we came and whither we were going) informed us we had wandered considerably out of our road . . . During the whole of this conversation, we could not avoid remarking that the woman appeared to be very uneasy; but when he offered to accompany us a little way in order to put us into the right road the distress of both was more perceptible, and the wife in particular seemed, by her gestures, to entreat him not to leave her. To these marks of anxiety, however, he only answered 'nonsense, nonsense', and extricating himself from the ladies who held him by the arm and coat he joined our party. On our enquiring the cause of this evident alarm on the part of the females, he informed us that our appearance had awakened their fears; that they had assured him we were either travelling robbers or prisoners who had broken from gaol; that the packs on our backs were full of the plunder we had picked up, and without doubt we should rob and murder him when we had seduced him from his dwelling.

J . . . n had taken with him from home a map of North Wales and a small pocket compass, and it was now we found their utility and importance. By showing and explaining these to our conductor, he marked out what course we were to make for, since everything like a path had long since faded away, and nothing but untrodden heath was before us. We therefore rewarded the confidence of our guide with a handsome present, and took leave of him; who, after giving us very particular directions, many blessings, and shaking us heartily by the hand, (a token of kindness which these mountaineers never fail to offer) committed us to the wild hills of Merionethshire.

Richard Warner: A Second Walk Through North Wales (1798)

Theodore Watts-Dunton
(1832-1914)

This critic and novelist is little read today, but in his lifetime he enjoyed some success. He was deeply interested, as Borrow was, in Romany life and customs. In Wales he will be remembered as the author of Aylwin. *In this excerpt we find the first person narrator at Betws-y-coed.*

I walked in the direction of the Swallow Falls.

Being afraid that I should not get much privacy at the Falls, I started late. But I came upon only three or four people on the road. I had forgotten that my own passion for moonlight was entirely a Romany inheritance. I had forgotten that a family of English tourists will carefully pull down the blinds and close the shutters, in order to enjoy the luxury of candlelight, lamp-light, or gas, when a Romany will throw wide open the tent's mouth to enjoy the light he loves most of all – 'chonesko dood', as he calls the moonlight. As I approached the Swallow Falls Hotel, I lingered to let my fancy feast in anticipation on the lovely spectacle that awaited me. When I turned into the wood I encountered only one person, a lady, and she hurried back to the hotel as soon as I approached the river.

Following the slippery path as far as it led down the dell, I stopped at the brink of a pool about a dozen yards, apparently, from the bottom, and looked up at the water. Bursting like a vast belt of molten silver out of an eerie wilderness of rocks and trees, the stream, as it tumbled down between high walls of cliff to the platform of projecting rocks around the pool at the edge of which I stood, divided into three torrents, which themselves were again divided and scattered by projecting boulders into cascades before they fell into the gulf below. The whole seemed one wide cataract of living moonlight that made the eyes ache with beauty.

Aylwin (1898)

Herbert Williams

Herbert Williams is a poet, novelist, biographer and journalist. He is also a former BBC producer.

They'd reached the low country now, on the border of Wales. We wasn't sure exactly where he was, but he guessed it might be Herefordshire. Or Montgomery. His geography was a bit hazy.

He'd been tramping for weeks, picking up a bit of work here and there, dossing down in fields or barns, it didn't matter where. He'd been lucky with the weather. What he'd do when winter came he didn't know.

There were lots of things he didn't know any longer. He'd pushed them out of his mind.

The people were pretty kind, generally. The wartime spirit was still there. Sometimes they asked about him, sometimes they didn't. If they asked he told them. He'd done his bit and that's that. He didn't want to settle down. He'd seen enough.

The women were gentle with him as a rule. Some had sons still in khaki, waiting demob. They hoped they wouldn't end up like him; he could see it in their faces. Others were more his age. They gave him funny looks sometimes, as if they wouldn't be averse to. If he'd wanted it, they might have let him. But he didn't.

The Stars in their Courses (1993)

John Stuart Williams
(1920-2001)

River Walk, Cardiff

Walking by the river, the morning cold
thick between old trees
dimly spread in parkland ease,
he stops to watch a mess of small
boys, a muddy ruck of all-sorts,
playing at playing rugby, hurts
and triumphs muffled in the turf.
                    The ball,
kicked true for once, hangs
in the lifting wind, gull without wings,
then drops dead in his unused hands.
The feel of it, the dubbined skin, sends old
signals through his fingers, cold
and clumsy, releases things long forgot,
the smell of wintergreen, the hot roar
of crowds, running in to score,
a snatch of rude song: a scene
that mocks the years in between, fall
of leaf, the cruel quickness of it all.

A clatter of startled rooks breaks
him free: he grins, wryly kicks
the ball back, resumes his steady walk.

Virginia Woolf
(1882-1941)

Virginia Woolf was staying at Manobier in Pembrokeshire in 1908. The letter from which the following extract is taken was addressed to her sister Vanessa Bell.

. . . I walked along the Cliff yesterday and found myself slipping on a little ridge just at the edge of a red fissure. I did not remember that they came so near the path; I have no wish to perish. I can imagine sticking out one's arms on the way down, and feeling them tear, and finally whirling over and cracking ones head. I think I should feel as though I saw a china vase fall from the table; a useless thing to happen without any reason or good in it. But numbers of people do fall over . . .

The Flight of the Mind; *The Letters of Virginia Woolf,*
Vol 1, 1882-1912
edited by Nigel Nicholoson and Joanne Trautmann (1975)

William Wordsworth
(1770-1850)

Wordsworth formed a close friendship with Robert Jones as a young man and as a result spent some four months in his household, Plas-yn-Llan at Llangynhafal in the Vale of Clwyd in 1791. This was his base for walking tours to other parts of North Wales. He and Jones ascended Snowdon from Beddgelert by moonlight and Wordsworth was inspired to write of the experience in his autobiographical poem The Prelude.

In one of these excursions, travelling then
Through Wales on foot, and with a youthful Friend,
I left Bethkelet's huts at couching-time,
And westward took my way to see the sun
Rise from the top of Snowdon. Having reach'd
The Cottage at the Mountain's Foot, we there
Rouz'd up the Shepherd, who by ancient right
Of office is the Stranger's usual guide;
And after short refreshment sallied forth.

It was a Summer's night, a close warm night,
Wan, dull and glaring, with a dripping mist
Low-hung and thick that cover'd all the sky,
Half threatening storm and rain; but on we went
Uncheck'd, being full of heart and having faith
In our tried Pilot. Little could we see
Hemm'd round on every side with fog and damp,
And, after ordinary traveller's chat
With our Conductor, silently we sank
Each into commerce with his private thoughts:
Thus did we breast the ascent, and by myself
Was nothing either seen or heard the while
Which took me from my musings, save that once
The Shepherd's Cur did to his own great joy
Unearth a hedgehog in the mountain crags
Round which he made a barking turbulent.
This small adventure, for even such it seemed
In that wild place and at the dead of night,
Being over and forgotten, on we wound
In silence as before. With forehead bent
Earthward, as if in opposition set
Against an enemy, I panted up
With eager pace, and no less eager thoughts.
Thus might we wear perhaps an hour away,
Ascending at loose distance each from each,
And I, as chanced, the foremost of the Band;
When at my feet the ground appear'd to brighten,
And with a step or two seem'd brighter still;
Nor had I time to ask the cause of this,
For instantly a Light upon the turf
Fell like a flash: I looked about, and lo!
The Moon stood naked in the Heavens, at height
Immense above my head, and on the shore
I found myself of a huge sea of mist,
Which, meek and silent, rested at my feet:
A hundred hills their dusky backs upheaved
All over this still Ocean, and beyond,
Far, far beyond, the vapours shot themselves,
In headlands, tongues, and promontory shapes,
Into the Sea, the real Sea, that seem'd

To dwindle, and give up its majesty,
Usurp'd upon as far as sight could reach.
Meanwhile, the Moon look'd down upon this shew
In single glory, and we stood, the mist
Touching our very feet; and from the shore
At distance not the third part of a mile
Was a blue chasm; a fracture in the vapour,
A deep and gloomy breathing-place through which
Mounted the roar of waters, torrents, streams
Innumerable, roaring with one voice.
The universal spectacle throughout
Was shaped for admiration and delight,
Grand in itself alone, but in that breach
Through which the homeless voice of waters rose,
That dark deep thoroughfare had Nature lodg'd
The Soul, the Imagination of the whole.

Wordsworth returned to north west Wales with his wife and daughter in 1824. In a letter dated September 20th he wrote to Sir George Beaumont.

In the afternoon there being no carriage-road, we undertook to walk by the Pass of Llanberis, eight miles, to Capel Cerig; this proved fatiguing, but it was the only oppressive exertion we made during the course of our tour. We arrived at Capel Cerig in time for a glance at the Snowdonian range, from the garden of the inn in connection with the lake (or rather pool), reflecting the crimson clouds of evening. The outline of Snowdon is perhaps seen nowhere to more advantage than from this place. Next morning, five miles down a beautiful valley to the banks of the Conway, which stream we followed to Llanrwst; but the day was so hot that we could only make use of the morning and evening.

LITERATURE FROM WALES

- ### THE FRENCH THING
  A novel by Chris Keil to the backdrop of the western Welsh agricultural crisis and livestock exporting.
  ISBN: 0-86381-768-8; £7.50

- ### THE LILY AND THE DRAGON
  A historical novel after Agincourt by Dedwydd Jones.
  ISBN: 0-86381-752-1; £9.50

- ### BIG FISH
  by Jon Gower
  Lively, entertaining short stories.
  ISBN: 0-86381-619-3; £6.95

- ### RARE WELSH BITS
  by John Williams
  A strange and compelling melange of tales.
  ISBN: 0-86381-700-9; £4.50

- ### GREAT WELSH FANTASY STORIES
  Ed. Peter Haining
  ISBN: 0-86381-618-5; £6.90

- ### CAMBRIAN COUNTRY
  by David Greenslade
  Creative essays on Welsh emblems.
  ISBN: 0-86381-613-4; £5.75

- ### THE LITERARY PILGRIM IN WALES
  by Meic Stephens
  A guide to places associated with writers in Wales. 266 places; 415 writers.
  ISBN: 0-86381-612-6; £6

ANTHOLOGIES FROM WALES

- ### WALES A CELEBRATION
  An anthology of poetry and prose. Ed. Dewi Roberts
  ISBN: 0-86381-608-8; £6

- ### FOOTSTEPS: an anthology of Walking in Wales.
  Ed. Dewi Roberts. *ISBN: 0-86381-774-2; £5.50*

- ### SNOWDONIA, A HISTORICAL ANTHOLOGY
  Ed. David Kirk; *ISBN: 0-86381-270-8; £5.95*

- ### AN ANGLESEY ANTHOLOGY
  Ed. Dewi Roberts. *ISBN: 0-86381-566-9; £4.95*

- ### BOTH SIDES OF THE BORDER
  An anthology of Writing on the Welsh Border Region. Ed. Dewi Roberts
  ISBN: 0-86381-461-1; £4.75

- ### GREAT WELSH FANTASY STORIES
  Ed. Peter Haining
  ISBN: 0-86381-618-5; £6.90